MW00579426

Toward a Common Future

Toward a Common Future

Ecumenical Reception and a New Consensus

William G. Rusch

CASCADE *Books* • Eugene, Oregon

TOWARD A COMMON FUTURE
Ecumenical Reception and a New Consensus

Cascade Books
An Imprint of Wipf and Stock Publishers
199 W. 8th Ave., Suite 3
Eugene, OR 97401

www.wipfandstock.com

PAPERBACK ISBN: 978-1-5326-5169-4
HARDCOVER ISBN: 978-1-5326-5170-0
EBOOK ISBN: 978-1-5326-5171-7

Cataloguing-in-Publication data:

Names: Rusch, William G.

Title: Toward a common future : ecumenical reception and a new consensus / by William G. Rusch.

Description: Eugene, OR: Cascade Books, 2019 | Includes bibliographi-
cal references and index.

Identifiers: ISBN 978-1-5326-5169-4 (paperback) | ISBN 978-1-5326-
5170-0 (hardcover) | ISBN 978-1-5326-5171-7 (ebook)

Subjects: LCSH: Ecumenical movement | Church unity

Classification: BX8.3 .R47 2019 (print) | BX8.3 2019 (ebook)

Manufactured in the U.S.A.   05/20/19

Pro illa quae scit
et erat apud me

Contents

Preface

THE PURPOSE OF THIS book is really quite simple. It is to offer a way for churches divided by centuries of disputes, disagreements, and even at times hostility, to move from their divisions and polemics towards a conception of visible unity that Scripture attests is the will of the Lord of the church.

Throughout the centuries, and especially in the twentieth and twenty-first centuries, a number of churches have participated in the modern ecumenical movement. This multifaceted movement has at its center both the task to the churches and the gift from the Triune God to challenge and urge the churches to move beyond their divisions. This movement has had some remarkable successes. Yet after more than a century of the modern ecumenical movement, churches remain divided even if much of the polemic and caricature found in history has been removed.

Recently it seems that the movement toward church unity has stalled. Building upon the past efforts of the search for unity, and especially the theological dialogues between the churches, this volume seeks to identify and supply a way for the churches to regain the momentum that appears to have been lost in the last few decades. It will finally be for the churches themselves to determine the validity of the approach pictured in the following pages. I hope that at least it will receive serious attention and debate.

For more years now than I care to recall, I have been active in the ecumenical movement and reflected about its promises and disappointments. In the process, I have written much. Now I find that to make a case for the argument of this book, I must set the context for this new proposal. In this undertaking, I have returned to the content of a number of items that I have published earlier. The material rehearsed here is not for the sake of mere repetition. Its goal is to provide for the reader the necessary background to understand and appraise a new approach to address church-disunity. It is in that spirit that the early chapters are included.

As is appropriate, the first chapter is devoted to an explanation of the modern ecumenical movement. The second and third chapters describe the history of the movement. The fourth chapter pictures the present challenge to the ecumenical movement from the perspective of the dialogues. The fifth chapter treats ecumenical reception. The sixth chapter presents a recent ecumenical concept. The seventh chapter explains a new type of ecumenical document and gives an example. The last chapter, the eighth, summarizes the conclusions of the argument put forth in the preceding pages.

This volume could not have been written without the support and scholarly contributions of many who have labored before me. Especially mention must be made of Professor Harding Meyer, not only a dear friend but a scholar and theologian of the ecumenical movement without peer. The following pages have profited from the careful attention of another close friend, Dr. Norman A. Hjelm. This contribution to the unity of Christ's church would not have reached its published form without the efforts of someone who wishes to remain anonymous and yet embodies the aspirations of this volume.

William G. Rusch
Reformation Day, 2018

1

The Modern Ecumenical Movement— What is It?

Its Goal—Its Basis

THE PURPOSE OF THIS volume is to propose a solution to one of the pressing challenges facing the languishing "modern ecumenical movement." Adequately to understand this proposal assumes some knowledge of what the ecumenical movement is—its goal and its basis. Such knowledge reveals why this movement is not merely one option among many but is critical to all churches as they seek to be faithful to their calling.

What is It?

Much of the twentieth-century history of Christianity could be described by this expression, the modern ecumenical movement. This phrase and what it signifies, however, has often been misunderstood or even rejected by members of churches that ostensibly are committed to the intention of ecumenism. Exploration of what this movement seeks to accomplish will necessitate a clear understanding of this four-word formulation, "the modern ecumenical movement."

Attaining a precise picture of this movement is a more complicated task than it might appear at first glance. Augustine of Hippo's comment about time is apropos: everyone knows what time is until it needs to be defined.[1] Likewise, everyone knows what the ecumenical movement is until a description is needed. The process of articulating an accepted description has been long and even now remains ongoing.[2]

For present purposes, the following definition is offered: The modern ecumenical movement is a search for unity in truth as found in Jesus Christ. It is a search for the will of God in every area of life and work that seeks to discern, proclaim, and participate in the Triune God's eternal and constant purpose for humankind and the mission of God to the world. It is a movement of people, which exists at global, regional, and local levels.[3]

This definition of the modern ecumenical movement has a number of implications flowing from it. First, this ecumenical movement is exactly that, a movement. It is not primarily an institution, although it exists in institutional forms. Second, it involves individuals committed to a vision of the oneness of the church. The movement may be composed of churches, but in its origin and in chapters of its history, churches were not the predominant participants. Third, as a movement, it has experienced periods of crisis. Fourth, it is multidimensional in that it includes education, mission, and concern for issues of peace and the alleviation of poverty and racism. Fifth and most importantly, at its center and influencing all else is a commitment to the gift and task of expressing the *visible unity of the church of Jesus Christ*.[4] This fifth implication can appropriately be considered the goal of the entire movement.

1. See Augustine, *Confessions*, XI, xiv (17).

2. See the documentation and comments in Kinnamon, ed., *The Ecumenical Movement*, 71–115; and also in Kinnamon, "Assessing the Ecumenical Movement."

3. I have constructed this definition of the "modern ecumenical movement" from the characteristics of the movement presented in the *Dictionary of the Ecumenical Movement*, edited by Lossky et al., xvi–xvii. See also Rusch, "Tradition," forthcoming.

4. In 1985 I argued that this core understanding of the ecumenical movement is essential to its very nature. In intervening years there is much evidence that erosion of this understanding has occurred in many places with the result that ecumenism today is often seen merely as cooperation between divided churches. See Rusch, *Ecumenism*. See also more recently Tjørhom, "The

Its Goal

Accordingly, this goal provides motivation and meaning to all the other aspects of the movement. Without a central commitment to this goal, the modern ecumenical movement runs the risk of losing its essential objective and focus. The choice of this goal is not arbitrary. It is embedded deeply in the origins of the ecumenical movement, reaching back to the early years of the twentieth century. It acknowledges that the ecumenical movement is concerned with one of the four classical characteristics or marks of the church—"one," unity.

This goal means that the ecumenical movement must never be indifferent to questions of ecclesiology—what is the church? Agreement in ecclesiology is a prerequisite for any expression of the visible unity of the church. Such a consensus allows and even encourages a proper diversity. This recognition is now part of an ecumenical understanding that moves beyond the early stress on organic union.[5]

In this connection the word *visible* or the concept of *visibility* is significant. While the word *visible* does not always appear in early documents of the ecumenical movement, the idea of *visibility* is clearly present. The concept of *visible unity* preserves two key thoughts: it maintains the distinction between God's action as a gift and the human response as a task; and it insists that this unity is a visible, empirical reality of Christian existence and action. So the movement is a movement toward "*visible* unity."[6] It is described as the "*modern* ecumenical movement" to distinguish it from other efforts for unity of the churches prior to the twentieth century.[7]

The centrality and significance of this goal of the *visible unity of the church of Jesus Christ* have been matters of debate and

---

Demise of Visible Unity."

5. See Meyer, *That All May be One*, 4–47 and 94–101.

6. For a rationale for the centrality of the visible unity of the Christian church in a proper understanding of the modern ecumenical movement, see Rusch, *Ecumenism*, esp. 1–18; and Meyer, *That All May be One*, esp. 7–15.

7. See Rusch, *Ecumenism*, 19–25.

even disagreement in the ecumenical movement, especially since the 1960s. Often the World Council of Churches has been the locus for the discussion of these views.[8] Yet the World Council of Churches has not been the only place where concern about the goal of the movement has been addressed. In 2016 Cardinal Kurt Koch, the President of the Vatican's Pontifical Council for Promoting Christian Unity, wrote of the present situation in which this central and historic purpose of the ecumenical movement has become endangered.[9]

It must be recognized that the language of "visible unity" has been problematic for some individuals and churches in the ecumenical movement. There has been a concern that "visible unity" requires a unified church organization, the question being: how does this "visible unity" relate to the "invisible unity" of the church? The relation of the visibility and invisibility of the church has been a topic of discussion for centuries. At the present time some churches regard "visible unity" as unnecessary or even undesirable because they consider the church by its nature to be "invisible." Other churches, such as the Roman Catholic Church and the Orthodox churches, believe that the visibility of the church exists in them. In spite of such concerns and reservations, churches have joined or related to the World Council of Churches, the constitution of which holds up the goal of visible unity.[10] Churches have also participated in dialogues with other churches when such dialogues have called for visible unity between them. The unavoidable conclusion seems to be that these concerns about "visible unity" do not obviate the participation of many church bodies in the one ecumenical movement.

Even with this consensus about the final goal of the modern ecumenical movement—the "visible unity of the church"—questions

8. See Chapter Two below.

9. Koch, *Information Service*.

10. Constitution of the World Council of Churches III/I. See also the statement of the Council's Central Committee, "The Church, the Churches, and the World Council of Churches" (Toronto, 1950): " . . . it is a matter of simple Christian duty for each church to do its utmost for the manifestation of the Church in its oneness . . . ," in Kinnamon, ed., *The Ecumenical Movement*, 420.

about the nature and form of this unity persist. Indeed, there are issues about the specific terminology to be employed, e.g. "organic unity," "reconciled diversity," or "communion of communions." Such differing terms and models should not be seen as in conflict; rather, they can be mutually reinforcing, allowing different Christian groups with their own diversities to affirm their membership in the one church.

During the course of the modern ecumenical movement four models of unity have enjoyed prominence: organic unity, conciliar fellowship, reconciled diversity, and communion of communions. Each of these models has its own history.

"Organic unity" was the original goal of the Faith and Order movement. It involved the death and rebirth of many forms of church life that now exist and the creation of a new church that would express the fullness of Christ's church in a particular place.

"Conciliar fellowship" is not so much a model of full visible unity as it is a picture of how "organic unity" could be lived out among different local churches. Local churches with different locations and cultural backgrounds could express their unity in councils of representatives of local churches. The Fifth Assembly of the World Council of Churches, meeting in Nairobi in 1975, gave definition to this concept.

"Reconciled diversity" affirms present confessional difference and their need to continue. These differences are not simply to be preserved and maintained, however, but they are to lose their divisive character and be reconciled to each other. Two assembles of the Lutheran World Federation, the Sixth Assembly at Dar es Salaam in 1977, and the Seventh Assembly at Budapest in 1984, gave support to this model.

"Communion of communions" provides that the various confessions would continue, albeit within the context of a larger ecclesial allegiance that would reflect common dogma and a basic ordering of ministry. The concept was proposed by Johannes Willebrands, who subsequently became the President of the Vatican's Pontifical Council for Promoting Christian Unity. Within this structure the Bishop of Rome would exercise a unique ministry in the service of unity.

The commitment to "visible unity" in whatever model or combination of models is not simply an argument for expedience or efficiency, although in some ecumenical literature it has been presented or understood in that way. Rather, the dedication to the "visible unity of Christ's church" on the part of the modern ecumenical movement is strongly anchored in the teaching of Scripture.[11]

Its Basis

Already in the Hebrew Scriptures there was a realization of God's desire that God's people express a unity of community, and not be simply a collection of individuals. The Hebrew word for people, *am*, appears over 1,500 times in those Scriptures. In point of fact, the expression "people of God" is understood as a technical term for Israel as God's chosen people. The people of God in the Hebrew Scriptures becomes a designation of a diverse but united group whose purpose is to be God's means of witness to the nations.[12]

This interpretation is obvious in Genesis 12, where Abraham is called by God to create a great, varied, and united people who through Abraham are to be a blessing to all the nations of the earth. This theme of unity and diversity is not lost in subsequent stories of the twelve patriarchs where the pattern for the origin of the twelve tribes (Gen 49) is given. It is these twelve tribes of the one people who become the basic structure by which God—in both old and new covenants—offers his plan of salvation. This pattern of the unity and diversity of "the twelve" is found in the New Testament with the twelve disciples. In the Old Testament, this organization reflects both the gathering into unity of one people and the diversity of each tribe in that unity.

11. The following review of biblical teaching on unity is indebted to Rusch, *Ecumenism*, 1–9, and Meyer, *That All May be One*, 7–15.

12. See also "The Significance of 'People of God' in the History of Salvation," in Kasper, *The Catholic Church*, 120–22.

The division of the people of Israel after the reign of King Solomon shows the same structure: diversity in two kingdoms and unity in that both the Northern kingdom and Judah are understood to be one people of God. There are two kingdoms, but they are united in their worship of the same God, exhibiting the unity willed by God.

This vision continues under the prophets, who call God's chosen but unfaithful people back to their mission of unity. The prophets speak to a people that has broken its covenants with God. For example, it is Third Isaiah who seeks to restore the broken unity of Israel so that Israel may be a light to the nations, extending God's salvation throughout the world (Isa 60). This same call appears in Ezekiel (Ezek 20:34, 34:12–13) and Hosea (Hos 14). God brings judgment on God's faithless people but God also provides a promise of reconciliation. It is in this setting that the concept of a remnant becomes significant: a small group, a remnant of the faithful, will be the witness to God's love of and concern for all nations.

The message of the Hebrew Scriptures regarding the people of Israel is obvious. God creates a united and diverse people to be his witness to the nations. Both characteristics are important. Even in the light of continuing sin, God intends through this diverse and difficult people who yet are one to show his love for humankind.

Over the course of this multi-century history, it is striking that there is an absence of uniformity among this one people. Often, full agreement on critical matters is lacking. Unanimity does appear to exist—it occurs at the departure from Egypt, but by the crossing of the Red Sea and the covenant event at Sinai not all the later tribes are included. The unity of the people of Israel is never uniformity. The people are united in diversity as they assemble to worship the one God.

In the documents of the New Testament, there is both continuity with the picture provided by the Hebrew Scriptures and discontinuity in light of subsequent developments and changes. Statements about the church in the New Testament are not in the abstract but reflect specific historical situations. While there is not one timeless picture of the church, there is nevertheless the clear notion that the church is one. Even when "churches" are mentioned, the idea is of individual congregations that are part of the one church whether in Corinth, Rome, or other places. Although according to the Gospel accounts Jesus did not organize clearly defined communities, the immediate post-Easter community was profoundly influenced by salvation as understood in the Hebrew Scriptures with its apocalyptic expectation of the reestablishment of the people of the twelve tribes.

A critical phase commences with the decision of the so-called "Hellenists" to begin a long process of moving Christianity beyond the Jewish people thereby separating itself from Jewish religion (Acts 7, 8). The book of Acts and various letters in the New Testament offer a picture of Gentiles becoming disciples without becoming Jewish proselytes.

The New Testament gives a picture of change not only in ecclesiology but in eschatology, soteriology, and anthropology. The rule of Christ under the Spirit is the source of a unity, but it is a unity in diversity, certainly never a sterile uniformity. Life and fellowship in the Holy Spirit have tensions and differences—as between Jewish Christian and Gentile Christian churches, between Paul and the enthusiasts at Corinth, between John and an emerging catholicity. This can be seen in the various theologies preserved in the New Testament.[13]

For example, the Apostle Paul sees unity at the center of his theology. This is no doubt because he sees the unity of the church closely related to his Christology, his understanding of Christ. Paul uses images such as "people of God," "temple of God," and "body of Christ" in association with discussions about baptism and the Lord's Supper (1 Cor 10:17; 12:12 seq.). There is one Christ for all, Jew and Gentile. Thus there is one gospel of salvation (Gal 1:6–9). Through his Christology and soteriology, Paul defends the unity

13. See Daniélou, *A History of Early Christian Doctrine Before the Council of Nicaea*, Vol. One: *The Theology of Jewish Christianity*, and Vol. Two: *The Gospel Message and Hellenistic Culture*; and Dunn, *Unity and Diversity in the New Testament*.

of the church. When the unity of the church is threatened, correct Christology and soteriology are endangered.

Nevertheless, Paul also acknowledged that considerable diversity does not destroy the unity of the church. Different organizational patterns in the churches of the New Testament did not challenge their unity. Even in the area of Christology uniformity was not demanded (Gal 2:1–10). Paul must have known that the original Jewish Christian communities used titles such as *Messiah, Son of Man,* and *Servant of God* as key christological expressions. The Hellenistic communities and Paul himself preferred terms such as *kyrios* and *Son of God* as christological expressions. Paul's care for the collection for the church in Jerusalem shows his concern for the unity of the church that includes communities beyond those that he established. (1 Cor 16; Gal. 2:10).

Concern for the unity of the church is also apparent in the Gospels. While the Gospel of Mark does not employ the word *ecclesia*, there are warnings about appearances of false Christs and prophets in the end times that affect the unity of the community (Mark 13:22). The issue of unity is present in the Gospel of Matthew in a somewhat less obvious form. The church spreading through the known world had to refer back in a clear way to Jesus of Nazareth. The founding of the church on Peter and the delivery of the keys to the apostles suggest threats to the unity of the church, which in the view of Matthew is the true people of God, the new Israel (Matt 16:18 seq.; 18:18).

The Gospel of Luke and the book of Acts also give evidence of attention to the unity of the church. The so-called council of the apostles (Acts 15) takes up discussion about the unity of the church in the context of a community composed of Jews and Gentiles. The unity is seen in a community of God, a new people made up of Jews and Gentiles. This view is certainly present in the farewell speech of Paul (Acts 20). The idyllic picture, which may be less than totally accurate historically, reveals a community holding correct belief, keeping common worship, having a common ordering, and recognizing the authority of the apostles (Acts 2:42 seq.; 4:32 seq.; 5:12 seq.; 9:31; 15:20–17).

Questions of unity are present in the Johannine literature. The farewell prayer of Jesus (John 17) is a request for the unity of the church (John 17:11, 20–23). The Fourth Gospel as no other presents Jesus speaking directly and clearly to the concern for the unity of a community, a community that experiences its unity with God. According to Johannine theology, this unity cannot be established by institutions or dogma and be made visible. This unity is present only through the Word of proclamation where Jesus is present in his unity with the Father. There is no temporal disadvantage because the unity of believers is dependent upon belief in Jesus present through the Spirit. The understanding of succession in the Fourth Gospel plays a role here. Unity with Christ leads to a unity of believers. In the unity of the disciples is reproduced the unity of believers with the Father and the Son through the Spirit.

The above, brief survey yields several insights. First, the unity of the community, real or imagined, becomes an issue when false Christian teaching arises. Such teaching impairs the unity of the community. Yet this should not be understood in a way that makes New Testament unity only a matter of orthodoxy. That understanding of unity only becomes a factor by the middle of the second century, as witnessed to by the patristic writer Irenaeus. Also, the diversity of teaching recognized by Paul was not regarded in the New Testament period as a detriment to unity. This, however, should not lead to the conclusion that the unity of the church was completely independent from the teaching of the church—only as an invisible reality or an issue of eschatology.

Second, diverse teachings are not as such to be seen as an obstacle to the unity of the church. This is because unity is in the person of Jesus Christ whose word and work bring salvation to the world. For example, there is a difference in the discussion about the teaching of error in the Pastoral Epistles and 2 Peter from what is found in the Pauline letters. In the Deutero-Pauline letters, the Catholic Epistles, and Hebrews a great esteem for unity is present with different substantiation. The entire New Testament reflects an instructive diversity and unity. This diversity can even be seen as an enrichment if it accompanies accepted views of Christology and soteriology.

Third, although there is significant diversity in the New Testament, there is also a remarkable agreement on many aspects of unity. These aspects include the idea that unity is not to be seen as "a desirable feature" of life in the church. Rather, it is a *condition for the church's existence* since this unity is rooted in the church's one Lord who is present in every local community. Locality and universality are not played off against each other. The church may have many organs, but there is only one church. Diversity is to be acknowledged, but not division.

Finally, there is one conclusion to be drawn from the biblical texts: There is one church with a richness of diversity in theology, forms of worship, and structures. This church knows tensions and disputes, but divisions and large numbers of Christians separated from full fellowship with one another are not evident. *The fundamental conviction of the biblical witness is the essential visible unity of the church of Jesus Christ.* The dedication of the modern ecumenical movement to this unity is quite understandable in view of biblical teaching.

2

The Ecumenical Movement from Its Beginnings to the Present

Part 1

THE FIRST CHAPTER PROVIDED a definition and rationale—largely in biblical terms—for "the modern ecumenical movement." It argued that for this multifaceted movement the visible unity of Christ's church is central to its understanding and is its proper goal. This objective is to be seen in harmony with the teaching of Scripture, in which visible unity is portrayed as an indispensable element of the church's identity. To the degree that it is lacking, the church is less true to its essential nature. The initial chapter also indicated that this position regarding visible unity was not held unanimously by all even if they or their churches were willing to participate in the ecumenical movement.

The present situation of the modern ecumenical movement and the frustration that it causes for many can only be grasped by an awareness of the history of the movement from its beginnings in the early twentieth century to its most recent developments in the opening years of the twenty-first century.

In spite of the core commitment to visible unity in ecumenical thinking, history has revealed how ephemeral and elusive such unity has been. Even in the New Testament churches, it is evident that unity was fragile. In ensuing centuries lengthy periods of time demonstrate the visible disunity of Christ's followers. Churches, primarily in the East, during the early centuries of the Christian

era, were consumed with theological disagreements and contro-
versies about the understanding of the Triune God and the person
of Christ. After the Council of Chalcedon in the year 451 these
christological disputes became fixed in divisions that endured into
the twenty-first century.

The churches of the West and the East moved toward a rup-
ture that has perhaps been fixed too exactly to the year 1054. The
church in the West, having centered its unity around the papacy
for eons, experienced divisions in the sixteenth century over
long-simmering differences. Most of the protagonists in these
feuds had hoped that permanent breaches could be avoided even
though these fissions represented for their adherents serious
matters of faith and practice. Still, nothing like modern denomi-
nationalism had developed until the sixteenth-century divisions
in the Reformation.

Even with this tragic history, the importance of, and commitment to, visible Christian unity was not denigrated. The narrative
of the church's history of disputes and divisions has often been
recounted.[1] Such telling of the church's story reveals traces, often
slight and not always evident, of the profound concern of both
individuals and the churches themselves for the unity of church.
This unity has been perceived as God's will for the people of God.
An early example even in a time of severe polemic and division is
Philipp Melanchthon in the sixteenth century.[2] In the seventeenth
and eighteenth centuries persons like François de Sales, Georg Ca-
lixtus, William Wake, and Nicolaus Ludwig Zinzendorf expressed
great concern about Christian unity.[3]

1. See among many possible examples, Irvin and Sunquist, *History of the
World Christian Movement,* Vol. I: *Earliest Christianity to 1453,* and Vol. II:
Modern Christianity from 1453 to 1800. The present narrative of the early phas-
es of this history parallels the account in my earlier work, *Ecumenism,* 19–33.

2. The efforts of Philipp Melanchthon in the sixteenth century may be cited
as one example in this long history. See Kasper, *Luther,* and McNeill, "The Ecumenical Idea and Efforts to Realize It, 1517–1618," esp. 42–48 and 67–69.

3. See Schmidt, "Ecumenical Activity on the Continent of Europe in the
Seventeenth and Eighteenth Centuries," and Sykes, "Ecumenical Movements
in Great Britain in the Seventeenth and Eighteenth Centuries."

This situation changed in dramatic ways with the arrival of the nineteenth century.[4] Movements of the eighteenth century such as the evangelical awakening and global missionary endeavors flowed into the next century and increased in energy. The nineteenth century became a time of renewed emphasis on global mission, with its consequent geographical expansion of Christianity. These factors resulted in a revived interest in ecclesiology and the creation of worldwide denominational fellowships. Such developments inevitably led to considerations of the chief theme of ecumenism, viz., the unity of the church. Early in the century William Carey suggested a missionary conference of all denominations to gather in South Africa. C. F. A. Steinkot of the German Christian Fellowship at Basel had numerous contacts in a variety of churches. In 1846 the Evangelical Alliance was established when some 800 Christian leaders met in London. In 1844 and 1854 respectively the Young Men's Christian Association and the Young Women's Christian Association were founded.

These latter two organizations, together with the Student Christian Movement, would provide a seedbed for future ecumenical leaders. By the end of the nineteenth century, John R. Mott, an American Methodist layman, would become the founder of the World Student Christian Federation and be recognized in the twentieth century as a primary pioneer of the modern ecumenical movement.[5] By the end of the nineteenth century all these factors took on new urgency after centuries of Christian division, quarrels, and anathemas. They led to the catalytic event that is often viewed as the birth of the modern ecumenical movement.

Indeed, the origin of the modern ecumenical movement has often been located in the World Missionary Conference held in Edinburgh in 1910. This identification is certainly accurate, but in some ways the Edinburgh Conference should also be viewed as a summing up and bringing into focus of the various developments

4. See Yoder, "Christian Unity in Nineteenth Century America," and Brandreth, OGS, "Approaches of the Churches Towards each Other in the Nineteenth Century."

5. See Hopkins, *John R. Mott, 1865–1955*.

and events of the previous century. The Edinburgh Conference was a consultative gathering of Protestant mission societies. It had no legislative authority and was neither representative of all the churches nor of all the areas of the world. Yet the World Conference disclosed a new sense of fellowship among Christians, trained future ecumenical leadership, and supplied an inducement for future ecumenical developments. It cannot be denied that the scandal of Christian disunity on the global mission field of the nineteenth century was *a* major, if not *the* major cause, for the rise of the modern ecumenical movement in the twentieth century.[6]

In 1910 the Protestant Episcopal Church in the USA took formal action to encourage the appointment of a commission to bring about a conference on matters relating to "Faith and Order." The purpose of this conference was to address the theological issues standing in the way of Christian unity. Other churches took similar actions. The outcome of such recommendations was a series of international conferences on Faith and Order. The first conferences were held in Lausanne in 1927 and Edinburgh in 1937. The Second World War caused a temporary interruption in the activity of the Faith and Order movement.[7]

Almost simultaneously with the emergence of Faith and Order, another dimension of the modern ecumenical movement was being expressed.[8] In 1925 the first "Life and Work" Conference took place in Stockholm, Sweden. Under the influence of the Edinburgh Conference, the Lutheran, Nathan Söderblom, in 1914 promoted a program on "Peace and Christian Fellowship." After he became the Lutheran primate of Sweden he suggested, in 1920, a Universal Christian Conference on Life and Work. This vision came to reality in 1925 with the Stockholm Conference. The participants agreed that there should be cooperative work on the

6. See Stanley, *The World Missionary Conference, Edinburgh 1910.* Robert S. Bilheimer's *Breakthrough: The Emergence of the Ecumenical Tradition* is a personal and engaging account of this history through the 1960s.

7. See Tatlow, "The World Conference on Faith and Order."

8. See Ehrenström, "Movements for International Friendship and Life and Work"; and Jonson, *Nathan Söderblom,* esp. 363–74.

part of the churches to address issues of contemporary society. In 1937 at Oxford a second Conference on Life and Work convened. As in the case of Faith and Order, the work of Life and Work was suspended by the Second World War.

Even before the Second World War, the two parallel conferences on Faith and Order and Life and Work had, in the 1920s and 1930s, disclosed a growing convergence between the two movements as parts of the one ecumenical movement. The Oxford Conference on Life and Work approved a proposal for a "World Council of Churches" that would incorporate both Life and Work and Faith and Order. The Edinburgh Conference on Faith and Order meeting in the same year approved the proposal and elected a committee to work with the committee that had been selected in Oxford. In Faith and Order circles some reservations were expressed, among others about the ecclesial nature of the proposed World Council. These actions led to the establishment of a new "Provisional Committee of the World Council in the Process of Formation." Once again the Second World War provided an obstacle to ecumenical activity.

The World Council of Churches (WCC) was formally founded in 1948 at its first assembly in Amsterdam.[9] The theme was "Man's Disorder and God's Design." This first assembly revealed a clear desire of the member churches to come together and to seek unity and inner renewal. Even at this early date concern was expressed about social issues. After this date the World Council became the focus for most international ecumenical activity. In 1961 the International Missionary Council was incorporated in the Council's structures. Assemblies were held at approximately seven-year intervals.

The second WCC assembly met in Evanston, Illinois in 1954 under the theme, "Jesus Christ—the Hope of the World." The churches in Evanston affirmed their desire to grow together. They addressed social matters in the context of a world divided between Communist and non-Communist societies.

9. See Visser 't Hooft, *The Genesis and Formation of the World Council of Churches,* and "The Genesis of the World Council of Churches."

The third assembly gathered in New Delhi in 1961 with the theme, "Christ, the Light of the World." A number of Orthodox churches joined the Council at this assembly. The basis of the Council was changed so that the World Council was defined as a fellowship of churches that accept our Lord Jesus Christ as God and Savior. The assembly theme once again centered on issues of Christology, but the Asian setting of the meeting required attention to other major world religions.

The fourth assembly met in Uppsala, Sweden in 1968 and marked in a number of ways a shift in the focus of the Council. The earlier concentration on the visible unity of the church as the raison d'être of the ecumenical movement was largely replaced by attention to the changing world scene, economic and social development, the financial responsibilities of Christians, and the condemnation of racism. Everyone agreed that these were appropriate issues to be addressed, but some saw in this shift the movement turning away from its fundamental task.[10] It is obvious that subsequent assemblies of the Council were influenced by this shift. The structure of the Council reflected this change when in the course of time Faith and Order, one of the major movements in the formation of the World Council of Churches, became a sub-unit.

The fifth assembly of the WCC took place in 1975 in Nairobi, Kenya. The theme was "Jesus Christ Frees and Unites." "What Unity Requires" was an item on the agenda, but much attention was given to the relationship between the unity of humankind and the unity of the church, racism, sexism, and human rights. The search for a "just, participatory, and sustainable society" was a major topic of this assembly and the "Programme to Combat Racism" was reaffirmed.

The sixth WCC assembly was held in Vancouver, Canada in 1983 under the theme, "Jesus Christ—the Life of the World." It encouraged its member churches to engage in a "conciliar process of mutual commitment, or covenant, to justice, peace, and the

10. For a helpful discussion of this debate and its implications, see Pannenberg, "Unity of the Church." The Uppsala assembly itself is surveyed and its implications explored in Jonson, *Wounded Visions*.

integrity of creation, that included commitments to fight racism, sexism, caste oppression, economic exploitation, militarism, violations of human rights, and the misuse of science and technology." The churches were also asked to respond to the Faith and Order document, *Baptism, Eucharist and Ministry.*

The seventh assembly gathered in Canberra, Australia in 1991 with the theme "Come, Holy Spirit—Renew the Whole Creation." This was a different theme from earlier assemblies, and in it the question of discernment and linkage between Jesus Christ and the Holy Spirit was raised. The recent outbreak of the Gulf War disclosed deep differences within the member churches of the Council on the theory of "a just war." The Australian context provided a stimulus for a discussion of Aboriginal rights.

Harare, Zimbabwe in 1998 was the site of the eighth assembly, the theme of which was "Turn to God—Rejoice in Hope." This assembly marked the fiftieth anniversary of the World Council of Churches and was the largest assembly to date. The gathering took up issues of third world debt, human rights, and globalization. Issues of doctrine and ethics already raised in the Canberra Assembly and even earlier were also present in Harare. The Orthodox and other churches, however, reacted to a perceived lack of attention to these doctrinal and ethical subjects. Here was a resurfacing of the continuing debate within the ecumenical movement of the balance between theological and social concerns. A special commission was appointed at Harare to deal with these matters.

"God, in Your Grace . . ." was the theme of the ninth assembly, meeting in Porto Alegre, Brazil in 2006. Like former assemblies, this gathering was influenced by its immediate context, viz., in this case Latin America. The unity of the church, Christian identity, and religious plurality, economic justice, and overcoming violence were prominent themes on the assembly's agenda.

The tenth assembly gathered in Busan, Republic of Korea in 2013 with the theme, "God of Life, Lead Us to Justice and Peace." On its agenda were topics of justice and peace, and mission and bearing witness in today's world. Documents of the assembly included, among others, a statement on unity, the politicization of religions and the rights of religious minorities, the human rights of stateless people, and peace and reunification of the Korean peninsula.

This summary review gives some impression of the significant role of the World Council of Churches in international ecumenism. However, even in this area the World Council never had a monopoly. Already in the nineteenth century a number of worldwide fellowships of denominations were formed with considerable ecumenical implications.[11] These groupings continued in the twentieth century with such groups as the Baptist World Alliance, the Lutheran World Federation, and the World Alliance of Reformed Churches. These denominational associations largely, but not exclusively, emphasized justice and social concerns as opposed to topics of Faith and Order. The relationship of these world confessional families, or Christian world communions as they became known, to the World Council of Churches often became confused, marked at times by different understandings of the goal and purpose of the ecumenical movement.[12]

In addition and almost simultaneously, regional associations were developed. This grouping included such organizations as the East Asia Conference of Churches, the Conference of European Churches, and the All Africa Conference of Churches. Until the Second Vatican Council (1962–65) Roman Catholic participation in these regional councils of churches was almost nonexistent.[13]

Also, in the early twentieth century a number of national councils were created that largely bore the characteristics of regional expressions. They were usually Protestant in make-up and devoted chiefly to social issues. Examples would include the former British Council of Churches, the Canadian Council of Churches, and the National Council of the Churches of Christ in the United States.

---

11. See both Yoder, "Christian Unity in Nineteenth Century America," and Brandreth, OGS, "Approaches of the Churches Towards Each Other in the Nineteenth Century."

12. See Stransky, "Christian World Communions."

13. See Best, "Councils of Churches."

It is difficult to evaluate the impact of this conciliar dimension of the ecumenical movement. On the one hand, it has not resulted, after more than a century of activity, in the visible unity of the followers of Christ. This aspiration was clearly never realistic, although it was no doubt held by some, especially in its early years. Also recently, trends in conciliar ecumenism have become disturbingly apparent. Of greatest concern among these trends is actually the diminished role of councils of churches in the life of their member churches—and this includes the World Council of Churches. Such trends are marked by the preoccupation of churches with their own survival, even existence, and also by a number of social issues that even threaten new church divisions, as in the case of the many issues regarding human sexuality.

On the other hand, conciliar ecumenism has accomplished much. One outcome of the participation in councils by churches has been the removal of caricatures of each other. Polemics between churches have been reduced if not completely eliminated. A large degree of consensus on the social responsibility of Christians has also been achieved, albeit without complete agreement. In the conciliar context, churches have come to acknowledge that they share a given unity in Christ, expressed in a large, if not total, consensus in baptism, Eucharist, and ministry, in the understanding of the gospel as a message of God's grace and forgiveness, and in an acknowledgment of the Lordship and uniqueness of Jesus Christ.

In the previous account, a careful reading will disclose the notable lack of involvement of the largest church in the world, the Roman Catholic Church. In long sections of the narrative shared above, the Roman Catholic Church as church did not take part. Indeed, individual members of the Roman Catholic Church did play significant parts in the ecumenical story, but they did this as individuals.[14] In 1928, Pope Pius XI issued an encyclical entitled *Mortalium Animos,* which dealt with the question of "true religious union." This document is usually seen as an uncompromising

14. See Tomkins, "The Roman Catholic Church and the Ecumenical Movement, 1910–1948," and Vischer, "The Ecumenical Movement and the Roman Catholic Church."

rejection of Roman Catholic involvement in the modern ecumenical movement. According to its thought, Christian unity could only come with a return of non-Catholics to the one true church from which they had fallen away.[15]

Nevertheless there were also attempts within the Catholic Church to understand seriously the ecumenical movement without repudiating the encyclical. Father Max Pribella and Father Y. M. J. Congar addressed the issue of a "Catholic" ecumenism. Father Johannes Willebrands directed a Catholic Conference for Ecumenical Questions in the Netherlands. Still, in 1949 the Vatican once again published a document on the ecumenical movement, *De Motione Ecumenica*. This text acknowledged the importance of the ecumenical movement, but also declared that no Roman Catholic should attend ecumenical meetings without permission from the Vatican. Within approximately ten years this situation was to change dramatically.

In January of 1959 Pope John XXIII indicated his wish to call a council for the Roman Catholic Church. Between 1959 and 1960 staff at the Vatican worked at the task of constructing an agenda for the upcoming council. In 1960 the Pope created the Secretariat for Promoting Christian Unity, the name of which was subsequently changed to the Pontifical Council for Promoting Christian Unity. This office provided a place for regular contact between the Roman Catholic Church and other churches, and also with the World Council of Churches. In 1962 the Second Vatican Council opened. Delegated observers from almost all the Christian confessional families were invited to attend the Council. By the Council's conclusion some 186 such observers had taken part in the sessions of the Council, often having made suggestions regarding the drafting process of conciliar documents.[16]

15. On *Mortalium Animos,* see Tomkins, "The Roman Catholic Church and the Ecumenical Movement, 1910–1948," 682–84. On the other hand, Cardinal Walter Kasper sees a continuity in renewal between *Mortalium Animos* and the Second Vatican Council's document, *Unitatis redintegratio* of 1964; Kasper, *The Catholic Church,* 13. For an interesting perspective on this papal encyclical, cf. Jonson, *Nathan Söderblom,* 389–94.

16. See Velati, *Separati ma Fratelli.*

For purposes of this volume the most significant statement produced by the Vatican II was *Unitatis Redintegratio*, the "Decree on Ecumenism." This document was promulgated on November 21, 1964. In Chapter 1 a Catholic understanding of the fundamental invisible and visible unity of the church is set forth. This church "subsists in" the Roman Catholic Church, but is not coextensive with it. The practice of ecumenism is presented in chapter 2. The final chapter describes the two main historical divisions of the church, viz. between East and West, and within the West. Prayer, dialogue, and cooperation in pastoral work are viewed as the means of realizing full visible unity. This decree recognizes that the cause of ecumenism is indivisible. There is one ecumenical movement. The Second Vatican Council marked a profound shift in the Roman Catholic Church's relation to the modern ecumenical movement. Since then there has been no doubt about the entrance of this church into this movement. This irrevocably stimulated and changed ecumenism.[17]

In 2004 the American ecumenist Michael Kinnamon wrote, "It is difficult to know what overall assessment to make of the ecumenical movement from 1968 to 2000."[18] The sentence could easily be amended "to 2017." The difficulty in part is due to the fact noted earlier in this volume that the ecumenical movement is a multifaceted phenomenon. Progress has not been uniform across the many areas included in the movement. Another feature of the challenge is that as a movement, much in the ecumenical movement is not static but in flux. Nevertheless, it is possible to make some general evaluations after the last few decades.

First, if the primary goal of the modern ecumenical movement is the realization of visible unity of the church of Jesus Christ, it is obvious that in the early years of the twenty-first century this outcome has not been reached. Global Christianity is visibly

17. *Unitatis redintegratio* since its approval has occasioned a considerable literature. See Thönissen, ed., *"Unitatis redintegratio,"* and Cassidy, *Ecumenism and Interreligious Dialogue*. The full text of the Decree is found in Tanner, SJ, ed., *Decrees of the Ecumenical Councils*, Vol. II, 908–20.

18. Kinnamon, "Assessing the Ecumenical Movement," 51.

disunited. Yet that judgment standing alone is both too harsh and misleading. It overlooks the consequential progress that these disunited churches have made towards greater expressions of the unity they share in Christ.

In the initial decades of this century, most churches in the ecumenical movement placed behind them polemic and caricature, and entered into an era of cooperation and good will. One notable example of this, and not the only one, is the relation of Lutherans and Roman Catholics as the year 2017 began, marking the five hundredth anniversary of the Reformation. Among the notable events was a visit of Pope Francis to the Lutheran Cathedral in Lund, Sweden for a joint Lutheran-Roman Catholic service of prayer.

In the latter part of the twentieth century the ecumenical movement saw the expansion of its membership. The Roman Catholic Church and an increasing number of Orthodox churches became active participants in the movement. The distance between the ecumenical movement and several Pentecostal churches was reduced. Churches in the North and South, and East and West have established new relations within the context of the ecumenical movement. Churches have moved significantly together in their rejection of racism and sexism, often entering into areas of notable conflict. Involvement in the movement has led to new understandings of mission, new insights into the conduct of interfaith conversations, new and renewed concern for education, and made an influential impact on worship and spirituality. Churches on global, regional, and local levels have entered into memberships in councils of churches. Some churches have entered into church-union conversations and have actually surrendered their identity for greater expressions of organic union.

The modern ecumenical movement has also been attentive with some significant success to the types of theological disagreements that originally resulted in the division of the churches. Some immensely important illustrations of achievement in this area are *Baptism, Eucharist and Ministry*, the outcome of over fifty years of work by Faith and Order, and the *Joint Declaration of the Doctrine of Justification*, the product of almost fifty years of Lutheran-Roman Catholic dialogue.[19] Another achievement not to be overlooked is *The Church: Towards a Common* Vision also from the work of Faith and Order.[20] While of somewhat different character with more limited immediate results are the theological agreements between Oriental and Eastern Orthodox churches on Christology. Also to be mentioned is the large consensus among many churches about baptism, the nature of the apostolic faith, and decision-making.[21]

Still, the statement is true: the churches in the ecumenical movement remain divided. How is this to be explained?

As indicated in the past, there are some reasons for this continuing situation that can to some degree be justified.[22] For churches to move from disunity after centuries to any expression of unity requires profound changes in theology, self-understanding, and at times structures. Such modifications are neither facile nor quick. They challenge all concerned, laity and clergy, to humility and repentance.

Also, the relatively short history of the ecumenical movement must be kept in sight. Most major divisions among the churches are centuries old, if not millennia in length. The modern ecumenical movement is a little over 100 years old. Patience can never be an excuse, but patience has some claim to legitimacy.

In addition, new questions have appeared on the ecumenical agenda that were not present in the first years of its history. Recent decisions by divided churches on such topics of social justice—for example, human sexuality, and racism—require exploration as to whether or not they have church-dividing character.

Questions have arisen about how much agreement is needed for expressions of visible unity. The relationship of the unity of the church and the renewal of human community stands in need of

19. *Baptism, Eucharist and Ministry*, and *Joint Declaration on the Doctrine of Justification*.

20. *The Church*, Faith and Order paper 214.

21. Such topics will be taken up more completely in a subsequent chapter.

22. See Rusch, "What is Keeping the Churches Apart?"

further clarification. This is also true in regard to the final goal of the ecumenical movement: the visible unity of Christ's church. How does this finally get described?

Not to be overlooked is the internal condition of many of the churches in the ecumenical movement. There are serious disagreements that affect their internal unity. Many of these churches have also experienced a decline in membership and resources. When such conditions prevail, commitment to the unity of the church universal is sometimes viewed as a luxury and not a necessity. The slowness of the process toward visible unity, noted by many, is rooted in some existential factors.

However, this will not explain totally the present ecumenical environment. There is much justification for the talk about "the winter of ecumenism" or "the stagnation of ecumenism." There is also in the churches an unwillingness to take ecumenism seriously. The churches could courageously and faithfully take action at the present time to put a number of their divisions behind them. Yet that action is largely absent.

3

The Ecumenical Movement from
Its Beginnings to the Present

Part 2

THE FIRST TWO CHAPTERS of this volume have endeavored to accomplish several things. They have offered a description of the modern ecumenical movement and a partial narrative of its history. In these earlier sections allusion has been made to ecumenical dialogue, which is an essential component of this story. The purpose of this chapter is to more closely examine ecumenical dialogues in the context of the modern ecumenical movement. Our attention will be directed specifically to the Lutheran-Roman Catholic dialogue and consideration will be given to conclusions of this dialogue for the sponsoring churches. What are the implications of these conclusions for the future relations of the churches involved? This question has ramifications for other dialogues in addition to the Lutheran-Roman Catholic dialogue, and this examination can be seen as a case study.

"Dialogues" in this context are generally defined as religious/ theological conversations between divided Christian churches or groups designed to arrive at better understanding, or to overcome or avoid division. For example, the Council of Florence (1438–45) could be viewed as an instance of Greek Orthodoxy and Roman Catholicism engaging in dialogue in order to restore unity between two parts of the Christian Church. At the time of the Reformation in the West, there were such "dialogues" between Catholics and Lutherans. The Marburg Colloquy (1529) and the Regensburg [Ratisbon] Conference (1541) are two notable examples. There were also "dialogues" between Lutherans and Anglicans, and Lutherans and Reformed. Usually such bilateral (involving two partners) efforts in the sixteenth century had little practical effect on the relations between the participating partners.

In the beginning of the twentieth century, early in the modern ecumenical movement, bilateral dialogues occurred between several groups, including Anglicans and Roman Catholics, Anglicans and Orthodox, Anglicans and Old Catholics, and Lutherans and Reformed. The concrete results of such conversations were slight in terms of actual outcomes. The official relations between the churches involved saw little change.

Bilateral dialogues, as a category of ecumenical activity, subsequently were eclipsed when considerable stress was placed on multilateral conversations (involving more than two partners). This situation was especially true in the work of Faith and Order Movement and after the establishment of the World Council of Churches in 1948.[1]

This situation only changed in the 1960s when bilateral dialogues again became prominent. The explanation for this shift has often been seen as twofold. First, the multilateral work provided the context for churches with a new sense of confidence to enter directly into conversations with each other. Second, the Roman Catholic Church, which had come into the ecumenical movement as a result of the Second Vatican Council, had a strong sense of self-identity and gravitated toward churches that had a clearly defined theology, structured worship, and distinctive practice. From the Roman Catholic perspective, these bilateral dialogues allowed the Catholic Church to relate on a one-to-one basis with other churches. Here in bilateral dialogues was a place to explore, and perhaps even resolve, the theological issues that divide two churches or traditions.

This Roman Catholic preference also influenced other churches that became more open to exploring their differences

1. See Gassmann, "Faith and Order."

through bilateral arrangements. These churches saw in such dialogues the possibility for in-depth study of church-dividing issues. They also regarded the official character of these dialogues as providing a certain degree of authority to their work. Thus there was an encouragement to take the dialogues with a measure of seriousness beyond that of the conclusions of individual theologians working independently.

The doctrinal agenda of such dialogues supported the view that theological differences, which originated in earlier centuries, were still determining the relationships between churches of the present day. These differences must be confronted and resolved if visible unity among churches is to become a reality. Bilateral dialogues became a place of preference for such exchanges of views and suggestions for resolution. For many in the ecumenical movement, moreover, an explanation of this adjustment from multilateral dialogue to bilateral dialogue must recognize the work of the Holy Spirit.

The result of this change of focus has been a virtual explosion of dialogue activity on global and local levels. The literature produced from this dialogue work has become such that it is beyond the ability of any one individual to master fully its content. To take account only of dialogue reports on the international level there are now in English four volumes of several hundred pages each.[2]

These bilateral dialogues generally shared two characteristics: They were official in the sense that members of dialogue groups were appointed by church authorities, and they were by and large concerned with doctrinal matters that had caused division in the past. It was seen as necessary that these issues of doctrine must be overcome for the establishment of some form of greater, visible unity. The dialogues were enriched by several factors: the scholarship which flowed from the modern liturgical movement, new insights in biblical and patristic studies that corrected overly simplistic views of the early church, and a deeper understanding of theological language that accounted for a variety of theologies in the New Testament and early church. These different theologies are not

2. See especially footnotes 4 and following below.

necessarily mutually exclusive. As a result of these elements many of the historically divisive teachings of earlier periods were able to be reevaluated, often with surprising outcomes.[3]

There is no question that for many the conclusions of this dialogue work have been astonishing. Topics that have caused divisions among Christians were being examined in a new light. The novelty of this situation in the 1970s, 1980s, and 1990s has largely been taken for granted in the twenty-first century. The expectation of ecumenical "breakthroughs"—for better or worse—has become commonplace and not particularly relevant. Other issues seem at the present time to be more church-dividing than the doctrinal issues of the past on which these dialogues have concentrated.

In this process the dialogues report to their sponsoring churches or ecclesial organizations. These official dialogues are never self-standing; for their life and work they rely on the entities that called them into being. Where they have found convergence or consensus they seek to move beyond such agreement, encouraging their sponsors to take some official action on these theological agreements. This challenge has led directly into the area of *ecumenical reception* which will be examined in a following chapter.

A comprehensive survey of the bilateral dialogues since the 1960s is beyond the dimensions of this volume. Yet something of value can be gained by even a superficial summary of a collection of volumes devoted to international dialogues. The limits of this exercise must be recognized. There is a temporal dimension and a restriction to international dialogues. This means that many highly significant regional and national dialogues cannot be considered here.

Growth in Agreement: Reports and Agreed Statements of Ecumenical Conversations on a World Level was published in 1985 and comprises 514 pages.[4] It contains a useful general introduction to the theme of "dialogue" and the reports from thirteen dialogues,

3. See Quanbeck, *Search for Understanding*, 9–54; Rusch, *Ecumenism*, 69–73; and Maffeis, *Ecumenical Dialogue*, 49–104.

4. Meyer and Vischer, eds., *Growth in Agreement*. A useful resource for this early period is Ehrenström and Gassmann, *Confessions in Dialogue*.

including the Faith and Order text, *Baptism, Eucharist and Ministry.* The Introduction describes many of the agreements as new and pioneering, and points to the volume of material produced. The thirteen dialogues reflect the wide range of conversations that have been carried on: Anglican, Baptist, Disciples, Lutheran, Orthodox, Reformed, Methodist Old Catholic, and Pentecostal dialogues or conversations. Since most of these texts were produced in the 1970s and 1980s, this collection is a confirmation of the impact of the Second Vatican Council on bilateral dialogue activity.

The second volume in the series discloses the acceleration in the dialogue process in the 1980s and into the 1990s. *Growth in Agreement II: Reports and Agreed Statements of Ecumenical Conversations on a World Level, 1982–1998* is 941 pages in length.[5] It includes materials from twenty-nine dialogues, materials from the Joint Working Group between the Vatican and the World Council of Churches, and two World Council of Churches documents. The range of participating churches or church traditions is extensive. It includes the Adventist, Anglican, Baptist, Disciples of Christ, Eastern Orthodox, Lutheran, Methodist, Old Catholic, Oriental Orthodox, Pentecostal, Reformed, and Roman Catholic churches or traditions. Clearly in this period, bilateral dialogues had become a major activity of the ecumenical movement.

This pace did not markedly slacken in the subsequent period. *Growth in Agreement III: International Dialogue Texts and Agreed Statements, 1998–2005* presents 615 pages of material.[6] Again the same scope of participants is represented: Adventist, Anglican, Baptist, Disciples of Christ, Eastern Orthodox, Lutheran, Methodist, Mennonite, Oriental Orthodox, Pentecostal, Reformed, and Roman Catholic churches or traditions. The texts of the Joint Working Group between the Vatican and the World Council of Churches and the statement of the World Council of Churches Assembly in Brazil in 2006 are also part of this collection.

The continuing rate of dialogue activity is documented by the most recent publication in the *Growth in Agreement* series. *Growth*

5. Gros, FSC, Meyer, and Rusch, eds., *Growth in Agreement II.*
6. Gros, FSC, Best, and Fuchs, SA, eds. *Growth in Agreement III.*

in Agreement IV was published in 2017 in two volumes that comprise 1,034 pages of texts.[7] The division of material is somewhat different from the previous volumes. *Growth in Agreement IV, 1* is divided into two sections: material from Eastern Orthodox and Oriental Orthodox dialogues and dialogues with Roman Catholic materials. *Growth in Agreement IV, 2*, has three sections: texts from churches of the Reformation tradition, materials produced by the Faith and Order Commission of the World Council of Churches, and reports and documents from the Joint Working Group between the Vatican and the World Council of Churches. The two volumes present a total of thirty-seven documents that reveal new dialogue partners and a wider circle of participating churches in comparison to the previous volumes.

When the four volumes are considered together, several conclusions become apparent. In sheer quantity the ecumenical movement has produced a corpus of theological literature of significant proportion. As should be expected, the quality of scholarship in this body of material varies. Nevertheless, the overall judgment must be that these texts are impressive and merit careful study. They must also be recognized for what they are: a new type of theology, not based on any one Christian tradition, but forged out of discussion and reflection between different traditions. This means that previous standards of discernment must be used with caution or abandoned. The proper question is not: is this text sufficiently Orthodox, Reformed, or Roman Catholic (to take some random examples), but does this text reflect the faith of the church throughout the centuries? There is also the important fact that with very few exceptions, this material, commissioned and sponsored by the churches or their ecclesial organizations, has not been evaluated by their sponsoring entities.

On the basis of this overview, and in light of the purpose of the present volume, it is appropriate to give special attention to

---

7. Best, Fuchs, SA, Gibaut, Gros, FSC, and Prassas, eds. *Growth in Agreement IV, 1* and 2.

documents/texts from the Lutheran-Roman Catholic dialogue. There are a number of reasons that justify this.[8]

First, the two major traditions that participated in the initial sixteenth-century division of the Western church are involved. It was from the Lutheran-Roman Catholic split of that century that subsequent divisions in the West occurred, both from the Roman Catholic Church and within Protestantism.

Second, the Lutheran-Roman Catholic dialogue is one of the longest continuing bilateral conversations within the modern ecumenical movement, originating on the international level even prior to the conclusion of the Second Vatican Council.

Third, both in terms of the quantity and the quality of its work, this dialogue has been generally recognized as exemplary.

Fourth, it is one of the very few bilateral dialogues whose work received official action by the sponsoring churches, viz., the *Joint Declaration on the Doctrine of Justification*. Yet this one official act also points to the fact that there remain numerous other topics addressed by this dialogue that have not received official evaluation.

Since the mid-1960s Lutheran-Roman Catholic dialogue has taken place on the international level and in several national contexts. The description of the dialogue offered here will be largely restricted to the international and American dialogues.[9] This limitation should not be interpreted to mean that significant theological work was only accomplished in these two settings.

While the Second Vatican Council was still meeting, one Lutheran observer proposed to Roman Catholic authorities the idea of an international Lutheran-Roman Catholic dialogue. Soon, this idea set in motion planning for both an international and an America Lutheran-Roman Catholic dialogue. A "Joint Working Group" composed of persons appointed by the Lutheran World Federation and what was then the Vatican's Secretariat for Promoting Christian Unity recommended an international dialogue. This

8. For a recent survey of the international Lutheran-Roman Catholic dialogue, see Birmelé and Thönissen, eds., *Auf dem Weg zur Gemeinschaft*.

9. See Rusch, "Introduction to the American Edition," 4–7.

dialogue met for the first time in 1967 and published its first text, a wide-ranging document, in 1972, known both as the *Malta Report* or *The Gospel and the Church*.[10]

This text was followed by a number of other dialogue reports. In 1978 *The Eucharist* was published, which argued for a consensus between Lutherans and Roman Catholics on eucharistic presence and sacrifice.[11] The next dialogue publication was *Ways to Community*, which offered a description of the purpose of the dialogue.[12] A critical topic for future relations, the mutual Lutheran and Roman Catholic recognition of ministries, was the theme of *Ministry in the Church* of 1981.[13] *Facing Unity* from 1984 suggested a process which over time could result in the establishment of a joint Lutheran-Roman Catholic ministry.[14]

The dialogue noted in 1980 the four hundred and fiftieth anniversary of the Augsburg Confession by releasing the text, *All Under One Christ,* which documented the ecumenical promise of this Lutheran Confession.[15] Three years later, in 1983, the five hundredth anniversary of Luther's birth, the dialogue published *Martin Luther—Witness to Jesus Christ.*[16] This document, largely indebted to contemporary Roman Catholic study, offered an understanding of Luther and his thought that transcended earlier polemical pictures of the Reformer.

The dialogue report, *The Church and Justification,* was issued in 1994.[17] This text was particularly significant in that it examined the ecclesiological implications of this doctrine that was critically central to the Reformation. Twelve years later in 2006, *The Apostolicity of the Church*, which was entitled a "study document," by

10. See Meyer and Vischer, eds., *Growth in Agreement,* 168–89.

11. Ibid., 190–214.

12. Ibid., 215–40.

13. Ibid., 248–75.

14. Gros, FSC, Meyer, and Rusch, eds., *Growth in Agreement II,* 241–47.

15. Meyer and Vischer, eds., *Growth in Agreement,* 241–47.

16. Gros, FSC, Meyer, and Rusch, eds., *Growth in Agreement II,* 438–42.

17. Ibid., 485–565.

means of historical survey explored this topic.[18] This text is also noteworthy in that it recognizes the positive influence of the *Joint Declaration on the Doctrine of Justification* (1999) on Lutheran-Roman Catholic dialogue efforts.[19]

As the five hundredth anniversary of the Reformation approached, the dialogue released in 2013 *From Conflict to Communion*.[20] Like earlier dialogue texts that noted anniversaries, this document addressed the difficult task of now to note in an ecumenical age an event that divided the Western church. It described new perspectives on Luther and the Reformation and gave a historical sketch of the Lutheran Reformation and the Catholic response to it. The text drew attention to themes in Luther's theology addressed in the dialogue, called for a common commemoration of baptism, and suggested five ecumenical imperatives. *From Conflict to Communion* was intended to be a study for parishes and a resource for church members to learn of the dialogue. It offered no proposals to change the relationship of the two churches. Nevertheless, it is a document of considerable importance, and would have been unthinkable without the prior fifty years of dialogue on many levels.

Thus the dialogue from its inception in the 1960s until 2013 created some 544 pages of dialogue reports and statements. As this literature is examined, it is clear the initial stages produced shorter texts. As the dialogue progressed and took up more complex topics the documents became longer as did the interval between reports. Both of these features are hardly surprising.

On October 31, 1999, in Augsburg, Germany an event of unique ecumenical consequence occurred. Representatives of the Lutheran World Federation and the Vatican signed the

18. Best, Fuchs, SA, Gibaut, Gros, FSC, and Prassas, eds., *Growth in Agreement IV, 1*, 169–266.

19. For *The Joint Declaration on the Doctrine of Justification*, see the description later in this chapter.

20. *From Conflict to Communion* with introduction, study guide, and worship materials.

aforementioned *Joint Declaration on the Doctrine of Justification.*[21] This text is directly indebted to the activity of the Lutheran-Roman Catholic dialogue over its long history. It illustrates that the subscribing Lutheran and Roman Catholic churches have come to be able to express a common, albeit not total, understanding of the doctrine of justification by God's grace through faith in Christ. As a result of this common understanding the mutual condemnations of the sixteenth century between the Lutheran and Roman Catholic churches on this subject were judged no longer to apply to the churches in question. The *Joint Declaration on the Doctrine of Justification* is novel in the story of this dialogue. It is the only instance of official action taken by the sponsoring churches of the dialogue's work.

In addition to this international dialogue, since the 1960s a number of regional and national dialogues have been active. Naturally, the national dialogue of greatest interest here is the dialogue in the United States. This dialogue has close parallels with the international dialogue and has in fact shared participants with that dialogue, most notably Professor George Lindbeck of Yale, who for some years was simultaneously the Lutheran co-chair of the international dialogue and a member of the USA dialogue.

The America dialogue, sponsored by the USA National Committee of the Lutheran World Federation and the Roman Catholic Bishops' Commission for Ecumenical Affairs, after two years of preparation began its work in 1965.[22] The US dialogue was conducted for Lutheran churches which comprised most of the Lutherans in the United States, including the Lutheran Church-Missouri Synod, which is not a member of the Lutheran World Federation. In order to gain confidence the dialogue initially selected easier topics and then moved on to the more difficult issues. It began with a report, *The Status of the Nicene Creed as Dogma of the Church,* published in 1965. One year later

---

21. Gros, FSC, Meyer, and Rusch, eds., *Growth in Agreement II*, 566–82. See also *The Joint Declaration on the Doctrine of Justification.*

22. See Rusch, "Introduction," *From Conflict to Communion*, 5–7.

came *One Baptism for the Remission of Sins.* The next year saw the release of *The Eucharist as Sacrifice.*[23]

In the 1970s the dialogue moved to the topics of Eucharist, papal primacy, and the related subject of authority and infallibility.[24] The next phase of the dialogue addressed the divisive issue of the sixteenth century: justification. In 1985 *Justification by Faith* was published.[25] This text influenced the *Joint Declaration* mentioned earlier in this chapter. The subject of sanctification was taken up in *The One Mediator, the Saints, and Mary.* This report appeared in 1992.[26] A modest report on Scripture followed in 1995. In 2005 the dialogue published its tenth statement, dealing with ecclesiology.[27] In 2011 the eleventh volume of the dialogue's work appeared.[28]

These eleven dialogue reports total an astonishing 2,617 pages of theological reflection on issues that have divided Lutherans and Roman Catholics for five centuries. When the work of the international dialogue is added to this figure, 544 pages, the sum total reaches the incredible amount of 3,161 pages. This figure does not include other Lutheran-Roman Catholic dialogues such as the dialogues in Germany, Finland, and Sweden, to mention only three others.

Clearly a corpus of this magnitude challenges the ability of any person to control its contents. And it must also be acknowledged that all this material is not on the same level. Still, this body of material represents the creation of a new type of theology, an ecumenical theology that Lutherans and Catholics in isolation from each other have not and could not create. It has a legitimate claim to be a novelty in theological literature. With careful analysis, these

23. See Empie and Murphy, eds., *Lutherans and Catholics in Dialogue I–III.*

24. See Empie and Murphy, eds., *Eucharist and Ministry; Papal Primacy and the Universal Church; Teaching Authority and Infallibility in the Church.*

25. See Anderson, Stafford, and Burgess, eds., *Justification by Faith.*

26. See Anderson, Stafford, and Burgess, eds., *The One Mediator, the Saints and Mary.*

27. See Skillrud, Stafford, and Martensen, eds., *Scripture and Tradition;* and Lee and Gros, FSC, eds., *The Church as Koinonia of Salvation.*

28. See Almen and Sklba, eds., *The Hope of Eternal Life.*

myriads of pages disclose many convergences and consensus on topics that throughout history and until recently were regarded both as church-dividing and irreconcilable.

These dialogue pages do not offer solutions to all the issues that have divided these two traditions. In and of themselves they do not lead to visible unity between these two churches. Much work needs to be done in areas in addition to dialogue. Yet the inexorable conclusion of individual church leaders and theologians is that these dialogues have performed an inestimable task in offering the Lutheran and Roman Catholic churches a resource to address their historic, church-dividing differences. There should be a deep sense of gratitude to the individuals who sacrificed time, energy, and talent to produce this gift for the churches.

The strength and advantage of this approach has been demonstrated in the Roman Catholic dialogue. Still this procedure has inherent weaknesses. They include the danger of the isolation of individual dialogues from each other. Is there a risk here of dividing the one ecumenical movement? Is consistency of theological position maintained across the landscape of many dialogues? For example, do Methodists say the same thing to Roman Catholics as they say to the Reformed? Do Roman Catholics take the same position in dialogue with the Orthodox as they do with the Lutherans? The list could go on.

In order to address this potential problem, since 1978 a series of forums on bilateral dialogues has met. These forums have both addressed the topic of consistency and shown that bilateral dialogues and multilateral dialogues have particular tasks. The various dialogues should be seen in a close relationship and not as competitors. Ten such forums have met since the initial gathering in 1978. The most recent forums were the ninth in 2008 in Breklum, Germany with the theme "Many Ways to Unity" and the tenth in 2012 in Dar es Salaam, Tanzania with the theme "International Dialogues in Dialogue: Context and Reception."[29]

29. The World Council of Churches has periodically published *Reports of Forum on Bilateral Conversations*.

With the exception of the *Joint Declaration on the Doctrine of Justification* described above, the sponsoring churches have taken no official action, positively or negatively, on the numerous recommendations and conclusions of this dialogical work. The present situation is not one of rejection; it is a circumstance of neglect. This brings us back to the present ecumenical state. How is this situation to be overcome?

4

A Present Challenge to the Ecumenical Movement from the Perspective of the Dialogues

THE FIRST FEW CHAPTERS have described the nature of the modern ecumenical movement, traced its history from the early twentieth century into the next century, and provided an overview of the development of the dialogues.

The topic of this chapter is to investigate a present challenge to the ecumenical movement. There are indeed a number of challenges facing this movement in the twenty-first century. Yet one such point of resistance to further advance is the lack of attention to the results of the bilateral dialogues. A result of this omission is that the reception of the dialogues' work into the faith and life of the participating churches has largely not taken place. This is especially acute in the instance of the Lutheran-Roman Catholic dialogue—in spite of the unique success of the *Joint Declaration on the Doctrine of Justification*.[1] Such is also the case in respect to other dialogues involving Protestant churches with Orthodox and Roman Catholic churches.

Recently much attention has been given to the present state of the modern ecumenical movement. Some of this reflection has no doubt been occasioned by the one-hundredth anniversary in 2010

1. Chapter 5 will deal with the subject of ecumenical reception and will show that this concept has been largely successful in dialogues involving churches that trace their origins to the sixteenth-century Reformation.

of the Edinburgh World Missionary Conference, widely regarded as the movement's founding event. Earlier chapters in this book have alluded to the contemporary situation of ecumenism. It must indeed be acknowledged that the condition of the ecumenical movement in the opening years of the twenty-first century is complex. Quick and simple generalizations about its health should be avoided. Nevertheless, some observations may be made.

First, at the present time there is much to celebrate ecumenically. Over the past 100 years a significant and ever-growing number of churches have become active participants in the ecumenical movement. The tally of churches that take part in local, national, and international councils of churches, whatever the exact legal name these organizations bear, is impressive and has increased over the years. Besides conciliar arrangements, a number of covenants exist between the churches, their dioceses, synods, and congregations. Although the variation in the basic documents of these arrangements is considerable, almost all affirm the basic ecumenical commitment to the visible unity of the church.

Second, churches in the movement have gained greater willingness and confidence to engage in the area of ecumenical work known as Life and Work. These churches have cooperated together in the areas of social justice and economic improvement. A patent example of this work is the project on "Justice, Peace, and the Integrity of Creation 1983" initiated under the auspices of the World Council of Churches at its assembly in Vancouver. This work was reaffirmed at the Eighth Assembly of the Council in Harare, Zimbabwe in 1998.

Third, a number of church unions have occurred that have resulted in united or uniting churches. These uniting churches may be within the same confessional family, as in the case of the Evangelical Lutheran Church in America and the United Methodist Church in the United States, or from different confessional families. Probably the most notable example of the latter is the Church of South India, which in 1947 united Anglican, Congregational, Methodist, and Reformed churches. But there are others, such as the United Church of Canada, formed in 1925, and the Evangelical

Church of the Union in Germany, which traces its origin to the early nineteenth century. All these examples of intra-confessional unions reflect organic union as a model of church unity, where individual confessional identities are sacrificed for a greater expression of the visible unity of the church.

Four, there are instances of agreements of full communion between churches of different confessional backgrounds. While these agreements are not examples of organic union, they can be expressions of the full visible unity of the church because of their characteristics that usually include some if not all of the following: a common confession of the Christian faith; a mutual recognition of baptism and a sharing of the Lord's Supper, which allows for an exchangeability of members; a mutual recognition and availability of ordained ministers; a common commitment to evangelism, witness, and service; a means of common decision-making; and a mutual lifting of any condemnations.

Specific examples in the United States of these agreements of full communion or agreements of commitment to full communion involve the Christian Church (Disciples of Christ), the Episcopal Church, the Evangelical Lutheran Church in America, the Moravian Church in America, the United Church of Christ, the Presbyterian Church (USA), and the United Methodist Church. These churches are not all in full communion with each other, yet when the agreements of full communion are viewed together, they form a network of church relations that would have been impossible without the ecumenical movement.[2]

Behind all of these developments is the reality of theological dialogue between divided churches. While it is true that the vast majority of these dialogues have not received any official response from their sponsoring churches or church-related organizations, it cannot be denied that over fifty years these dialogues have created a context for positive ecumenical developments.

However, this critical fact can easily be misleading. The inescapable conclusion remains: the full benefit of these conversations has not been achieved. As mentioned previously, the dialogues

2. See chapter 5 and its examples of ecumenical reception.

generally have not been rejected; rather, they have been *neglected* by the churches. The reasons for this sad state of affairs have been set forth in an earlier chapter. To understand this situation, it may prove useful to look more closely at one specific dialogue: the Lutheran-Roman Catholic dialogue. The rationale for this choice has also been explained earlier. This dialogue serves as a case study for the impasse that so often occurs in Protestant-Catholic dialogue.

The International Lutheran-Roman Catholic Dialogue

Chapter 3 included a short overview of the international Lutheran-Roman Catholic dialogue. Here it is necessary to document the conclusions and recommendations of each of the reports from this dialogue. The present purpose is distinct from the earlier summary. It should be observed that the following review is not itself intended to be exhaustive. The present focus is on the conclusions of these dialogue reports and the actions the participants in the dialogues have urged their respective bodies to take.

The first published report from the international Lutheran-Roman Catholic dialogue (the Joint Lutheran-Roman Catholic Study Commission) is entitled *The Gospel and the Church*, also known as the *Malta Report*. It was issued in 1972.[3] The document is far-ranging in its content, covering a number of subjects. The preface requests the sponsoring churches to study this dialogue report. The commission members indicate that they believe the report shows a noteworthy and far-reaching consensus between Lutherans and Roman Catholics. They note also that a consensus is developing on the doctrine of justification. Many of the traditional doctrinal disagreements are seen as losing their importance in the modern world. The text states that there are new possibilities for a common understanding of apostolic succession and that substantial convergences about ministry are becoming apparent. The document asks: are differences between Lutherans and Roman Catholics on ministry church-dividing today?

3. See *Report of the Joint Lutheran-Roman Catholic Study Commission on "The Gospel and the Church", 1972 ("Malta Report")*.

The report requests the churches to consider official action on certain topics. The Catholic members ask their church to examine recognition of Lutheran ministry. The Lutheran members, acknowledging that the question of Lutheran recognition of Catholic ministry is different, request the Lutheran churches to examine seriously the question of explicit recognition of the Roman Catholic ministerial office. The document suggests an exchange of pulpits and occasional acts of intercommunion and common celebration of the Eucharist. Four Catholic participants and one Lutheran issued disclaimers to certain aspects of the report. Some Catholics found the proposal for occasional intercommunion to be questionable.

As this description makes clear, the report from this first dialogue had certain hopes and expectations. There was a request that the sponsoring churches would study the report and its conclusions. There was also a carefully nuanced wish that the churches consider seriously certain official actions which would involve recognition and a change in relationship between the churches. In many ways the *Malta Report* was ahead of its time. Both partners, the Lutheran and Roman Catholic churches, took no action on its work. A number of individuals and churches, however, did offer reactions, which included questions about the *Malta Report*'s statements on Eucharist and ministry.

The next report from the international dialogue was released five years later in 1978 under the title *The Eucharist: Final Report of the Joint Roman-Lutheran Commission.*[4] The preface declares that the report is offered to the churches for discussion. It claims that agreement has been reached regarding significant points, and remaining questions can be clarified mutually. The preface also notes that reactions from individuals have raised questions particularly about the Eucharist and ministry. The report states that what Lutherans and Catholics can jointly confess should find a place in the life of the churches.

Part I deals with the joint witness of Lutherans and Catholics. Part II affirms a Lutheran-Catholic agreement on the issue

4. Meyer and Vischer, eds., *Growth in Agreement*, 190–214.

of the real presence of Christ in the Lord's Supper. Catholics and Lutherans should now see their positions on this subject as no longer one of opposition. In fact, ecumenical discussion has shown that the interpretation of the other is a challenge to the other's position. Convergence is recognized on several points and there is a clarification of a number of outstanding questions. The topic of eucharistic intercommunion is taken up and in this regard the report indicates that the ecclesiological ordering of ministry is a critical factor. Thus a joint celebration by Catholics and Lutherans is forbidden. Lutherans hold the view that an exchange of pulpits and common eucharistic celebrations can be recommended on occasion. Attention is given in the document to the liturgical forms of the Eucharist.

The concluding section of the report, Part III, reveals that the participants in this dialogue believe that they have demonstrated legitimate and significant agreement regarding the Eucharist. Using the word *reception*, they ask fellow Christians to examine and consider their reflections both to improve them where needed and to make them their own as far as possible. This text from the early phase of the dialogue discloses once again the conviction that the involved churches have a responsibility to form some judgment about the dialogue's conclusions.[5]

This concern is quite obvious in the next publication from the international dialogue, *Ways to Community,* issued in 1980.[6] As the title discloses, this publication sets forth a suggested path for the churches from disunity towards visible unity. Part I states that the goal of these dialogue efforts is a unity given in the word and work of the Lord. Such unity is a gift and it is already being realized through God's grace. This first section of the report describes the nature of the community of faith with reference to the Word,

5. It should be noted that during these years a Roman Catholic-Lutheran-Reformed Study Commission was also at work. In 1976 it published a document, *The Theology of Marriage and the Problem of Mixed Marriages.* While there was not a complete agreement on the call for reception of the report, there was consensus that the churches should seriously consider the report and a number of concerns that it identified.

6. Meyer and Vischer, eds., *Growth in Agreement,* 215–40.

sacraments, and ministry, noting differences in Lutheran and Catholic understandings of these topics. The form this community takes will be visible, diverse, and dynamic. Part II is concerned with the possible steps towards unity. There is an acknowledgement of the place both for gradual rapprochement and intermediate goals. The steps should include some practical actions. There is the clear hope that the churches will engage in some specific acts towards a greater expression of their unity.

In 1980 the international dialogue took advantage of the four-hundred-fiftieth anniversary of *Confessio Augustana*, the Augsburg Confession, the fundamental text of the Lutheran Confessions. It published a report with the title, *All Under One Christ: Statement on the Augsburg Confession by the Roman Catholic-Lutheran Joint Commission.*[7] This relatively brief text notes the anniversary and expresses the hope that this concise statement will hasten Christian unity. It portrays the historical situation that led to the composition of the Augsburg Confession, declaring also that after the Second Vatican Council and the experience of the dialogue there is in 1980 a new situation—there is a new sense among Catholics and Lutherans that they are "all under one Christ." The ecumenical purpose of the Augsburg Confession has been rediscovered. In consequence, this report urges the sponsoring churches to accept the findings of the dialogue. It explains that this request is based on the nature and contents of the Augsburg Confession, as well as the findings of contemporary biblical, patristic, historical, and doctrinal scholarship. All these efforts show a basic consensus between Lutherans and Roman Catholics on such topics as the Trinity, justification, understanding of the gospel, and the sacraments. This consensus is apparent even In Part II of the Augsburg Confession, where sharp differences were noted.

To be sure, the report acknowledges that open and unresolved questions remain. These are topics to be explored in the future, but the basic and broad consensus already identified by the dialogue gives hope that these issues will be settled in a way encouraging greater unity. The document concludes by noting that the future

7. Meyer and Vischer, eds., *Growth in Agreement*, 241–47.

cannot be simply a time of repeating and referring back to the Confession of 1530. A fresh articulation of the common faith of Catholics and Lutherans is needed. In the footnotes the work and contributions of the United States dialogue are referenced as is a joint Lutheran-Roman Catholic commentary on the Augsburg Confession issued to mark the anniversary.[8] Even this short text from the dialogue reveals a constant theme in the thinking of the dialogue participants: the necessity of the churches to take action on the conclusions of the dialogue.

The next publication from the dialogue, entitled *The Ministry in the Church*,[9] came in 1981. The document's purpose is to discuss the topic of ministry at greater length than was hitherto possible. It understands this subject in broad scope, treating God's saving act through Christ in the Spirit, the specific topic of ordained ministry with a historical summary, the function of ministry, the nature and uniqueness of ordination, apostolic succession, and the distinction between the episcopate and presbyterate.

The report then takes up the ecumenically urgent question of the mutual recognition of ministries. It describes the present situation, the differing Catholic and Lutheran positions on the question, and future possibilities. This final section is of special interest and importance for the focus of attention of this work. It speaks of the rapprochement reached between the Catholic and Lutheran churches, the importance of mutual recognition, and declares that the solution to the problem lies in a process by which the churches would reciprocally accept each other. As part of this process, the text requests that the churches study *The Ministry in the Church*, engage in a process of reception of the work of the previous dialogues on ministry, and make the process of ordination and installation of ministers correspond to the consensus that has already been achieved. The next step according to the document would be an incomplete mutual recognition that declares that the Holy Spirit is active in the ministries of each

8. Forell and McCue, eds., *Confessing One Faith*.

9. Meyer and Vischer, *Growth in Agreement*, 248–75.

church. Such action would be an important step toward the full mutual recognition of ministries.

The presence and content of this final section is further indication of the desire of the dialogue participants to see their work not merely as an academic or theological enterprise but as a vehicle to draw their churches closer to full visible unity. Members of the dialogue grasp the challenge this presents to the churches, but they obviously also see it as part of their responsibility to keep this issue before the churches. As we are seeing, this is a theme in all the publications of the dialogue.

Three years later, in 1983, the dialogue noted the five-hundredth-anniversary of the birth of Martin Luther with the text, *Martin Luther—Witness to Jesus Christ.*[10] This recognition is similar to the action that the dialogue took in regard to the Augsburg Confession, and it resulted in a document of a comparable genre. The text begins by indicating there is a new situation in 1983 in regard to Catholic and Lutheran thought about Luther. He is viewed as a witness to the gospel by both parties. A mutual understanding of the central concerns of the Reformation is acknowledged. The consensus of *All Under One Christ* is repeated. As the outcome of many factors, a movement from conflict to reconciliation is taking place. Luther's conflict with church authorities and his view of *sola Scriptura* are better appreciated. Although history cannot be redone, the negative consequences of history can be healed and this is especially true when the positive aims of the Reformation become a joint concern for Lutherans and Roman Catholics. Lutheran churches today have gratitude for Luther, but they also recognize his limitations. Roman Catholics have had a critical attitude to Luther, but contemporary Catholic scholarship has altered this view. Catholics today note that the Second Vatican Council implemented requests first expressed by Luther and other Reformers. The report concludes by observing that Luther's legacy calls Catholics and Lutherans to a common task of learning from Luther together. Unlike other dialogue publications thus far surveyed, *Martin Luther—Witness*

10. See Gros, FSC, Meyer, and Rusch, eds., *Growth in Agreement II*, 438–42.

to Jesus Christ does not ask for specific action from the sponsoring churches. This calls for two comments. First, the text is a different type of dialogue report than those dealing directly with doctrinal disputes. Second, the text does strongly imply that consensus about the theology of Luther should have an impact on future relations between the churches.

The concern for practical steps to overcome the division of Lutheran and Roman Catholic churches is discernible in the next publication from the dialogue, *Facing Unity* of 1984.[11] This dense text comprises about 40 pages with 174 footnotes. At the outset it reviews the history of the dialogue; indicating that the dialogue's goal is to attain the degree of unanimity required if the churches are to decisively advance from the present state of division to that of sister churches. For this to happen there must be clarity about the nature of a church unity that rejects both absorption and return. The goal is to offer the churches a structured model of fellowship. In the opening pages of the report there is a clear request for examination, with perhaps correction and supplementation, by the churches in order to bring the text to a position of authority in the churches.

Thus *Facing Unity* is one of the clearest examples to date of the dialogue urging the churches to discern and if possible, with improvements, receive its work. Part I deals with the concept of unity and models of partial and comprehensive union. Part II is devoted to the forms and phases of Catholic-Lutheran fellowship. It points out that growth in fellowship will come through mutual recognition and reception. It then turns to a discussion of the community of faith, the community in sacraments, and a community of service. It then sets forth a bold plan of stages leading to the exercise of a common ordained ministry between Lutherans and Roman Catholics.

The document acknowledges that the proposal is visionary and that many questions remain open. Yet it closes with a request that Christians other than Roman Catholics and Lutherans consider the suggestions of the document and add their reflections

11. Gros, FSC, Meyer, and Rusch, eds., *Growth in Agreement II*, 443–84.

to the ongoing process. There is no specific call in the conclusion for the churches to take action on *Facing Unity*. The text's explicit appeal for a word of discernment and a positive acceptance of certain structural steps toward visible unity is reflected throughout the document.

This goal and commitment are again evident in the next publication from the dialogue, *Church and Justification* of 1993. Its first sentence asserts that visible unity has always been the ultimate goal of this dialogue.[12] This is, to date, the most extensive and dense text to come out of the dialogue, some 70 pages with 396 footnotes. Such a text defies an easy summary. *Church and Justification* views itself as completing the third phase of the dialogue. The *Malta Report* is the first; *Eucharist, Ministry in the Church*, and *Facing Unity* together with the two texts dealing with the anniversaries of Luther and the Augsburg Confession are the second. *Church and Justification* seeks to formulate its themes in a way to disclose their implications for church fellowship. The focal point of the report is the mutual relationship between justification and the church. The text took seven years to reach its final form.

For purposes of this survey, the critical question is placed at the outset of the document: Does this report along with the publications from the second phase provide a sufficient consensus for the churches to take concrete steps toward visible unity?

Part I has as its subject justification and the church, stressing the close interconnection between the two topics. Part II addresses the abiding origin of the church. Part III describes the church of the Triune God. Part IV presents the church as recipient and mediator of salvation. It is in this section that attention is given to the significance of the doctrine of justification for the understanding of the church. Part V turns to the mission and consummation of the church. This lengthy text is a virtual Lutheran-Roman Catholic ecclesiology. It concludes with no word requesting official action by the sponsoring churches. No doubt its drafters considered such an overture superfluous in view of the strong statement at the outset of the document.

12. Gros, FSC, Meyer, and Rusch, eds., *Growth in Agreement II*, 485–565.

49

The next document to be reviewed has two claims to uniqueness. First, it is not strictly speaking a report from the international dialogue; it is, rather, the work of a separate group drawing on the results of several studies and dialogues. Second, unlike all other texts examined thus far, it does not request official action by the sponsoring churches. Rather it enjoys official approval both of the Lutheran Federation on behalf of its member churches and the Roman Catholic Church. *The Joint Declaration on the Doctrine of Justification* was signed by the appropriate officials of both the Federation and the Roman Catholic Church in Augsburg, Germany on October 31, 1999.[13]

This signing conferred upon the *Joint Declaration* the status of an official statement both of the member churches of the Lutheran World Federation and the Roman Catholic Church. This had never occurred before with work emanating from a Lutheran-Roman Catholic dialogue. The consensus expressed in the *Declaration* was now an agreement between the sponsoring churches or their international means of expression on the fundamental truths of the doctrine of justification. It was not merely the views of dialogue participants. Three previous texts offered the rationale for this unparalleled step. They are the *Malta Report*, described above; a 1985 report of the United States Lutheran-Roman Catholic dialogue, *Justification by Faith*;[14] a publication from a dialogue in Germany involving the Roman Catholic Church and the Lutheran, Reformed, and United Churches in Germany, *Condemnations of the Reformation Era: Do They Still Divide?*[15] Here was a report originating in dialogue work that did not need to plea for consideration by the appropriate churches for acceptance or reception at some level. The approval of the Lutheran World Federation and the Roman Catholic Church in 1999 was followed in subsequent years by the approbation of the World Methodist Council,

13. Gros, FSC, Meyer, and Rusch, eds., *Growth in Agreement II*, 566–82. An English-language edition of the statement was published in 2000.

14. Anderson, Stafford, and Burgess, eds., *Justification by Faith*.

15. Lehmann and Pannenberg, eds., *The Condemnations of the Reformation Era*.

the World Communion of Reformed Churches, and the Anglican Communion. In the intervening years, the *Joint Declaration on the Doctrine of Justification* has demonstrated how a bilateral consensus can in effect become a multilateral agreement.

Quite reasonably, such a fundamental and influential text as the *Joint Declaration on the Doctrine of Justification* has played a key role in subsequent Lutheran-Roman Catholic dialogues. This is apparent in the very next document from the years of dialogue published in 2006, *The Apostolicity of the Church*.[16] This work was ten years in the making, completing the fourth phase of the dialogues. It was offered to the sponsoring bodies and a larger readership with the hope that it would open up new perspectives and cast light on pathways toward full communion between Catholic and Lutheran churches. The report does not specifically request acceptance or official action. Without rationale, it describes itself as a "study document." This is the first time in the several reports from the international dialogue that this term is used. It is difficult to avoid the conclusion that here is an attempt to downplay the importance of this lengthy text of over 200 pages and 159 footnotes.

The document is divided into four parts.[17] Initially, an Introduction appears which provides a history of the dialogue that both acknowledges the special status of the *Joint Declaration on the Doctrine of Justification* and notes certain limitations on this study of apostolicity. Part I then addresses the apostolicity of the church in terms of its New Testament foundations, the commission of the Risen Christ, the promise of the Spirit, and apostolic structures and patterns of ministry. Part II provides a historical review of apostles and church from biblical texts to early and medieval interpretations. It declares there are shared fundamental conclusions and common understanding of these topics between Catholics and Lutherans. Part III is devoted to

16. See Best, Fuchs, SA, Gibaut, Gros, FSC, and Prasses, eds., *Growth in Agreement IV, Book 1*, 169–266.

17. For a fuller description of *The Apostolicity of the Church* and from a different perspective, see Rusch, "The History, Methodology, and Implications of *The Apostolicity of the Church*," 118–34.

apostolic succession and ordained ministry. It contains a review of ordained ministry from the early church to present Catholic and Lutheran teachings using a methodology with three elements: the use of Scripture, the insights of the *Joint Declaration on the Doctrine of Justification*, and the concept of differentiated consensus.[18] Part IV speaks of church teaching that "remains in the truth." It portrays two areas of Lutheran-Catholic agreement. First, there is an area of full consensus on the gospel of God's grace in Christ, the gospel in the church, and the authority of Scripture. Second, there is an area of reconciled diversity dealing with the canon of Scripture and the church, Scripture and tradition, and the necessity of a teaching office. At its conclusion the report offers no specific recommendations; it contains no request for any official action by the churches involved.

The American Lutheran-Roman Catholic Dialogue

The American Lutheran-Roman Catholic dialogue has revealed both similarities and differences to what has been noted in the international dialogue. From the outset, as the above discloses, the International Commission asked for study in and response from the churches. The initial phase of the American dialogue was more tentative. The actual dialogue itself, after a preliminary stage of informal conversations, began in 1965. The sponsors were the Roman Catholic Bishops' Commission for Ecumenical Affairs and the USA National Committee of the Lutheran World Federation. The Lutheran Church-Missouri Synod, although not a member of the Federation, was invited to send two representatives to the dialogue.

From the beginning, the decision was made to start with topics on which there might be large areas of agreement. The dialogue began its work with a study of *The Status of the Nicene Creed as Dogma of the Church*, discovering substantial agreement. The report was issued in 1965. The dialogue moved on in a second round

18. This concept is described and evaluated in chapter 6 below. The English and German texts differ in their terminology regarding this expression.

to *One Baptism for the Remission of Sins.* Here again, a consensus was found, although questions about the development of doctrine, especially as they relate to the teaching office of the church, were identified as critical topics for future investigation. The report was published in 1966. Encouraged by the findings of these earlier discussions, the dialogue took up a more divisive issue from the sixteenth century: eucharistic sacrifice. *The Eucharist as Sacrifice* was published in 1967. As these first three reports are examined, a number of factors become clear. The dialogue participants were surprised and overjoyed with the consensus they were finding. The concluding statements are modest; primarily reportorial. It is only the last report on the Eucharist that raises the question of people and leadership of the churches, testing what the dialogue has discussed and its conclusions.[19]

After three years of intensive work the dialogue published in 1970 its report on Eucharist and ministry. In this significant publication, the dialogue distinguished between "Ministry" as the task of the whole church and "ministry" as a particular form of service within and for the sake of Christ's church. It discovered agreement in three areas: the apostolic nature of ministry and Ministry, entry into Ministry by ordination, and the character of Ministry. As a result, the dialogue proposed a series of recommendations. The Roman Catholics asked their church to recognize the validity of ministry and Eucharistic administration in Lutheran churches. The Lutherans requested that their churches institute the same type of recognition of Catholic ministry and Eucharistic celebrations.[20]

Between 1970 and 1974 the dialogue focused its attention on papal primacy. It structured its efforts around the concept of a Petrine function in the life of the church. This function was understood as a particular form of ministry exercise by a person, office holder, or even local church with reference to the church as a whole. The dialogue found agreement on a number of points,

---

19. Empie and Murphy, eds., *Lutherans and Catholics in Dialogue I–III: I The Status of the Nicene Creed as Dogma of the Church, II One Baptism for the Remission of Sins, III The Eucharist as Sacrifice.*

20. See Empie and Murphy, eds., *Eucharist and Ministry.*

including that such a function under the gospel and with a responsibility to seek the unity of all Christians cannot be ruled out on the basis of the biblical evidence. The Lutheran members of the dialogue asked their churches to consider the possibility and desirability of a papal ministry renewed under the gospel and committed to Christian freedom. The Catholic participants requested their church to consider the possibility of a reconciliation that would recognize the self-governing Lutheran churches in the dialogue as sister churches which are entitled to some measure of ecclesial communion.[21]

The next topic explored by the dialogue was even more challenging: papal infallibility. The final report of 1980 makes mention of the reassessment of popular assumptions and theological interpretations about infallibility that have taken place since the Second Vatican Council. It clearly acknowledges the great problems this doctrine creates for Lutherans. The degree of consensus in this final report is obviously less than in the previous publications. The dialogue did succeed, however, in transforming a topic of long-standing debate and oppositions into an open and mutual search for truth. The concluding statement, sixty-eight pages in length, is cautious with both the Roman Catholic and Lutheran participants asking their churches to take certain practical steps to promote greater mutual understanding and openness in future investigations of this topic. The text states that the members of the dialogue realize that the implementation of even the suggested steps will be difficult.[22]

Throughout its work the dialogue had recognized the importance of the topic of justification by faith. The dialogue alluded to this subject, which played such a prominent role in the sixteenth-century Reformation, but never addressed it directly in the early phases of its activity. From 1979 until 1983, however, the dialogue studied the issue, central since the Reformation, of justification by

---

21. See Empie and Murphy, eds., *Papal Primacy and the Universal Church.*

22. See Empie and Murphy, eds., *Teaching Authority and Infallibility in the Church.*

faith.[23] In the common statement, the dialogue acknowledged that Catholics and Lutherans use different thought structures to express the truth of this doctrine. Yet the final report stated that Lutherans and Catholics shared a common affirmation that the entire hope of justification and salvation rests on Jesus Christ and on the gospel where the good news of God's merciful action in Christ is revealed. The report closed by noting that this statement was being submitted to Roman Catholic and Lutheran churches for study and with the hope that it will serve them as they recognize the need to make appropriate decisions in confessing their faith as one.

From 1983 to 1990 the dialogue discussed the topic of *The One Mediator, the Saints, and Mary*. The intention of this round of dialogue was to test the doctrinal implications of fundamental affirmations and material convergences from the previous round on justification. The time devoted to this subject and the final documentation of 397 pages both disclose the seriousness with which this topic was addressed. The common statement repeated the position from earlier dialogue reports upholding the unique mediatorship of Jesus Christ. It noted that Lutheran and Roman Catholic churches are still separated by differing views of the invocation of saints, and the Immaculate Conception and Assumption of Mary. In spite of these differences, the dialogue participants asked their churches to take certain steps. Lutheran churches could acknowledge that Catholic teaching about the saints and Mary in the documents of the Second Vatican Council does not promote idolatrous belief and practice; they are not opposed to the gospel. The Catholic Church is asked to acknowledge that in a closer but still incomplete fellowship Lutherans with their stress on Christ as the one Mediator would not be obliged to invoke the saints or to affirm the two Marian dogmas.[24]

The next publication from the dialogue was a departure from the previous reports. It is a short document of sixty-two pages devoted to the relation of Scripture and tradition from both Catholic

23. See Anderson, Murphy, and Burgess, eds., *Justification by Faith*.

24. See Anderson, Stafford, and Burgess, eds., *The One Mediator, the Saints, and Mary*.

and Lutheran perspectives. It offers a number of conclusions that Catholics and Lutherans can share while noting that differences of emphasis and doctrine remain. The purpose of the report is to bring together the more than twenty-five years of the American Lutheran-Roman Catholic dialogue as the sponsoring churches reflect about the next phase of the dialogue.[25]

The first fruit of the new phase of the dialogue appeared in 2005 with the publication of *The Church as Koinonia of Salvation: Its Structures and Ministries*. This common statement is noteworthy for its affirmation of the *Joint Declaration on the Doctrine of Justification* as a resource for continuing dialogue especially with its methodology of differentiated consensus. It also contains a number of specific recommendations for recognition by the sponsoring churches. There are nine recommendations centering on recognition of the reality and woundedness of Catholic and Lutheran ministries and churches.[26] Acceptance of any or all of these recommendations would bring the churches involved into a closer relationship and move them along the path to full visible unity.

From 2005 until 2010 the dialogue discussed the theme of the hope of eternal life. Its report took up the common Lutheran and Catholic hope, the common doctrinal heritage, disputes between Catholics and Lutherans on aspects of this subject, and offered a concluding section. Here again the methodology of the *Joint Declaration on the Doctrine of Justification* is followed. The work of earlier rounds of the dialogue provides a foundation. There are no requests for the sponsoring churches to take action in regard to this round of dialogue.[27] Whether this lack is to be explained by the nature of the topic or internal developments in 2009 within the Evangelical Lutheran Church in America regarding standards for ordained ministry cannot be ascertained from the dialogue publication.

25. See Skillrud, Stafford, and Martensen, eds., *Scripture and Tradition*.
26. See Lee and Gros, FSC, eds., *The Church as Koinonia of Salvation*.
27. See Almen and Sklba, eds., *The Hope of Eternal Life*.

Conclusions

From these two reviews of the international and national Lutheran-Roman Catholic dialogues, it is possible to draw several conclusions. First, the dialogues reveal an extended period of serious theological scholarship at the highest levels. Second, this work, undertaken with the official sponsorship of churches or church organizations, is not to be viewed as theological scholarship for its own sake. Its purpose is to be a resource for the churches to overcome with integrity their past divisions and to move toward relationships of full visible unity or full communion. Third, the dialogues conclude that the churches have a responsibility to evaluate their work, to accept it, amend it, correct it, or even reject it if they deem it faulty. They do not have the option to ignore it. Yet with one exception this is precisely what has been done.

Before moving on, however, the conclusions drawn from the Lutheran-Roman Catholic dialogue must be tested with other bilateral dialogues. This review, obviously and by necessity, must be concise. It is based on a random selection of a few dialogues, but its results seem to be accurate. Any final and definitive conclusions would require more extensive research. The findings of this restricted survey should not be assumed as true for every dialogue.

From the earliest phases of the work of the Anglican-Roman Catholic International conversations, that dialogue submitted its work to the churches for their response. This situation was especially true after its report on the Eucharist (1971), Ministry and Ordination (1973), and Authority in the Church (1976 and 1981). The dialogue endeavored to take seriously the comments, suggestions, and criticisms it received from individuals and groups by publishing three elucidations: in 1979 on Eucharist, on ministry and ordination in 1979, and on authority in the Church in 1981.[28]

The Lutheran-Methodist International Dialogue, conducted on behalf of the Lutheran World Federation and the World Methodist Council, published the results of its work in 1984 under the title, *Church: Community of Grace*. It contained specific

---

28. See Meyer and Vischer, eds., *Growth in Agreement*, 61–129.

recommendations that the churches declare and establish full fellowship in Word and sacraments, engage in cooperative efforts of witness and service in the world, and receive and use the results of this dialogue to seek the visible unity of all Christians.[29]

In the same year, 1984, the Anglican-Reformed International Dialogue, under the sponsorship of the Anglican Consultative Council and the World Alliance of Reformed Churches, issued its report, *God's Reign and Our Unity*. This report, dealing with life in the church, ministry, and sacraments, offered a series of recommendations to its sponsoring churches to enhance unity between the two traditions, identify reciprocal communion, and consider the formation of united churches.[30]

In 2001 the Roman Catholic Church through its Pontifical Council for Promoting Christian Unity and the World Methodist Council, by means of a joint international commission, released a report with the title, *Speaking the Truth in Love*. The publication took up ecclesiology, ministry, and the means of grace. This dialogue publication in its preface asks the sponsors of this dialogue to evaluate its work.[31]

Also in 2001, a dialogue between the Oriental Orthodox family of churches and the World Alliance of Reformed Churches submitted its work to the authorities in the Oriental Orthodox Churches and the World Alliance of Reformed Churches. The report dealt with Scripture, mission, ministry, and the sacraments. The dialogue participants requested the appropriate authorities to consider and act on the report.[32]

The Anglican-Orthodox Joint Doctrinal Discussion published its report in 2006, *The Church of the Triune God*. This report,

29. See Gros, FSC, Meyer, and Rusch, eds., *Growth in Agreement II*, 200–218. Some of these recommendations were actually acted upon years later in the United States when the Evangelical Lutheran Church in America and the United Methodist Church took action to enter into a relationship of full communion.

30. Gros, FSC, Meyer, and Rusch, eds., *Growth in Agreement II*, 114–54.

31. See Gros, FSC, Best, and Fuchs, SA, eds., *Growth in Agreement III*, 138–73.

32. Gros, FSC, Best, and Fuchs, SA, eds., *Growth in Agreement III*, 39–57.

devoted to church, Christology, and ministry, was offered to the sponsoring churches for study and reflection so that the churches will by God be drawn closer together. The conclusion states clearly that the goal of the dialogue is the reception by the churches of each other in ministry, church structures, and faith.[33]

The fundamental conclusion of this chapter is twofold: first, there is considerable evidence from a variety of dialogues over the years, including but not limited to the Lutheran-Roman Catholic dialogue, that the participants in the dialogues expected and have encouraged responses (approval, rejection, partial approval with suggestions for improvements) from their sponsors to their work, and second that by and large, with extremely few exceptions, most notably being in 1999 with the *Joint Declaration on the Doctrine of Justification* between Lutheran and Roman Catholic churches, this expectation has not been fulfilled by the churches or ecclesial organizations that initiated the dialogues.

33. See Best, Fuchs, SA, Gibaut, Gros, FSC, and Prassas, eds., *Growth in Agreement IV, Book 1*, 25–82.

5

What is Ecumenical Reception?

THIS BOOK, IN ITS first chapter, provided an explanation of the modern ecumenical movement. It argued that this multifaceted movement has at its center a core commitment to the visible unity of the divided churches of Christ. On the basis of the witness of Scripture this goal is seen as valid for its own sake. The second and third chapters offered a brief summary of the history of the modern ecumenical movement and an analysis of its state in the opening decades of the twenty-first century. While recognizing the significant advances and contributions of the ecumenical movement after a hundred-year history, these chapters pointed out that the present status of the ecumenical movement is one often of stagnation if not retreat from its goal of visible unity. A number of valid and invalid reasons were suggested for this circumstance.

Along with this inertia, the present ecumenical situation in terms of dialogue activity can be pictured as an inundation of riches, *embarrass de richesse*. The results and publications of the bilateral dialogues since the 1960s have obviously been prolific. The previous chapter in its review of these dialogues suggested a constant theme running not only through the Lutheran-Roman Catholic conversations, but others as well: the strong wish of the various dialogue participants to receive some evaluation of their work by the sponsoring entities so that this work may serve as a resource to assist the churches in the overcoming of their divisions. The chapter pointed out that little if any such evaluation has taken place.

The solution offered here for this problem proposes that two components have been lacking to address this dilemma. Inattention to these two items has largely contributed to overall ecumenical stagnation. They are the practice of ecumenical reception and the use of differentiating consensus. The present chapter will address the first theme, the following chapter the second.

The purpose of this fifth chapter is to identify and explain what appears to be a major contributing factor to the present dilemma of both ecumenical catalepsy and superabundance of results. This significant factor does not negate the presence of such minor factors as have been noted in previous chapters. In brief, the thrust of this chapter is that the lack of *ecumenical reception* of the specific dialogues is part of the most satisfying explanation for the condition of the ecumenical movement at the present time.

If the dialogues, and especially the bilateral dialogues, together comprise the major driving engine propelling the churches from visible disunity to visible unity, it is obvious that the neglect of their conclusions by the involved churches is a critical factor contributing to this languor or even at times retreat from earlier progress. This thesis requires explanation and defense.

The basic fact is that the churches in the ecumenical movement with few exceptions have neither *rejected* nor *received* the results of their dialogues with other churches. Rather they have *neglected* these findings. There are several reasons for this fact.

First, the churches are confronting a new situation that they have never encountered before.

Second, they are being asked to evaluate a theology they have created with other churches, often employing novel or strange concepts and vocabulary.

Third, this theology often challenges the churches at the heart of their self-identity and requires changes in their self-understanding.

Fourth, churches often do not have in their structures the means to engage in the necessary appraisal of recommendations from dialogues.

Fifth, even after the evaluations of such ecumenical recommendations, the question remains: how do the churches receive this work in an authoritative and binding manner?

All these questions raise a topic in theology that until the last fifty years or so has been largely neglected: *reception*. In several articles and two books, I have taken up this subject. I wish now to summarize that research as it relates to the ecumenical scene in the early twenty-first century.[1]

"Reception" as a concept is multidimensional. It has a referent in the area of legal scholarship where it refers to the transfer of Roman law into European jurisprudence, especially German law, at the end of the Middle Ages. Scholarly attention to this phenomenon began in the seventeenth century and has continued until the present.

"Reception" also appeared in the study of literature in the nineteenth and twentieth centuries with the concepts of *Wirkungsgeschichte* and *Rezeptionsgeschichte,* in which the interrelationship between the reader and the text is explored. In philosophy, reception has been employed to describe an intellectual and cultural change, notably in the work of Hans-Georg Gadamer, but there are other examples. This history is of interest and can even add some insight into the major concern here. Yet it is not the primary area of attention in this chapter.[2]

The present concern is about reception as an ecclesiological process. It is frequently indicated that reception precedes the church itself. This is certainly true in the sense that the church arose out of a continual process of reception. In the Old Testament it is possible to discern the motifs of receiving and re-receiving. Creation receives its being from God. Human beings receive God's revelation; Israel receives the covenant.[3]

1. See Rusch, *Reception* and *Ecumenical Reception.*
2. See Rush, *The Reception of Doctrine.*
3. See Rusch, *Ecumenical Reception,* 7–13.

The New Testament makes clear that Christ receives his mission from the Father. The church as the community of faith, as Paul reminds the Corinthians, receives the gospel from Christ himself. Despite differences of detail, the various books of the New Testament describe a process of reception that is not legalistic and formal, but is rather a glad process of receiving the good news of the gospel from the Lord himself. This is always an event of the Holy Spirit. In the biblical sense, reception is one of the main characteristics of the Christian faith itself often present without the specific words λαμβάνειν and δέχεσθαι, or the Latin terms, *receptio* and *recipere*.

In the pre-Constantinian period reception was primarily concerned both with the process by which certain writings were accepted into the emerging canon of Scripture and the process by which local and regional synods were made known and accepted by other local churches. The early church saw itself as a fellowship of churches involved in a reciprocal process of giving and taking from one another. In all these instances what is involved is not a juridical action but a spiritual process of reception by the entire community.

A new factor appears in the Constantinian and post-Constantinian eras, when the emperor becomes directly involved in the councils and synods of the church. Now, council decisions acquired the status of imperial law. Yet even here reception is a process where laity, monks, and church leaders participate together with an enthusiasm that would seem strange to many today. This reception was determined by two principal ideas: *consensio antiquitatis*, consensus in the apostolic faith, and *consensio universitatis*, consensus of the councils of the church by the universal church.[4] Without both forms of consensus, the decisions of any council had little chance of reception.

Reception in the early church took place in areas besides those of the decisions about the canon of Scripture or of councils. In the fields of liturgy and of local laws and customs, reception was moving forward. Implicit in the practice was an understanding of

---

4. See Rusch, *Ecumenical Reception*, 14–32.

the church as a community of local churches in fellowship, *communio*, with each local church having gifts to share and a faith to be handed down from generation to generation.

Some of these factors, notably an ecclesiology of local churches, did not continue in the West in the Middle Ages. The sixteenth-century Reformation was in part a reaction against the ever-increasing papal domination of the church. The Reformation itself caused the reception and non-reception of new documents like the Lutheran Confessions (*Book of Concord*, 1580) and the decisions of the Council of Trent (1545–63).

This general description of reception is true for the Eastern churches, as it is for the church of the West, although Orthodoxy considered reception in the light of a total ecclesiology, not limited to statements of the magisterium in legal categories. For the East, reception involved agreement with the faith of the church as the final authority. It is the fruit of the charismatic work of the Spirit. The Orthodox churches see in reception a dialectical relation between the laity and the clergy, both of whom have a critical role under the inspiration of the Spirit.[5]

The ecclesiastical process outlined here is a process that occurred before the rise of the modern ecumenical movement in the twentieth century. It is usually described as *classical reception*. This type of reception has several characteristics. Classical reception was never only the acceptance of theological texts from church councils. It was never merely a juridical process. Rather, reception always functioned as a continual process that in a sense predated the institution of the church. It includes the receipt of God's love in his Son as well as the acceptance of a history and a tradition. It involves the constant practice of interpretation and reinterpretation. This reception is not static, but is a lively process of the church drawing from the resources of the past to seize and accept the present activities of its loving Lord.

Classical reception as pictured here was seriously neglected in theological scholarship for many years. In 1977 Franz Wolfinger, in an important article, raised the question whether reception

5. See Rusch, *Ecumenical Reception*, esp. 23–32.

as a concept had been forgotten in the church.[6] Nevertheless only six years later in 1983, Thomas Ryan described "reception" as the "new holy word" of the ecumenical movement.[7] What caused this dramatic shift from oblivion to notoriety?

The answer to this question lies in Pope John XXIII's dramatic calling of the Second Vatican Council. As pointed out earlier, this council, among its many concerns, raised questions about the ecumenical movement and the Roman Catholic Church's relationship to that movement. Such topics as the conciliar nature of the church, and how such conciliar decisions are *received* in the church gained a new urgency that was not present before. The Second Vatican Council thus moved reception to the center of theological attention of the divided churches after years of neglect. It also, almost simultaneously, became a topic of interest in ecumenical circles.

This renewal of interest was largely characterized by concern with *conciliar* reception because of the Second Vatican Council. It looked back to the early church and the Orthodox churches as resources. Yet this attention had more than a historical motivation. There was an eagerness to see how reception could become a resource for enabling divided churches to move closer to unity.

Another factor was the Roman Catholic Church's reception of its own council, a process persisting some fifty or more years after the council itself. An open question remains: how should Catholicism receive the Second Vatican Council? A considerable body of literature developed quickly after Vatican II in both Roman Catholic and ecumenical groups. In the intervening years such scholarship has continued.

In this context a new notion of reception emerged, viz., *ecumenical reception.* This category arose in the virtual explosion of bilateral theological dialogues between the divided churches. There is no doubt that the Second Vatican Council was the catalyst for this new situation. It is ecumenical reception that has occasioned the series of questions raised at the outset of this chapter.

6. See Wolfinger, "Die Rezeption theologischer Einsichten und ihre theologische und ökumenische Bedeutung."

7. See Ryan, "Reception."

Attention in the reminder of this chapter will be given to the concept of ecumenical reception. Suffice it to say, as demonstrated in the previous chapter, the dialogues beginning in the late 1960s and early 1970s, and continuing to the present, in an ever-persistent manner have pressed their sponsoring churches or church-organizations to undertake this new kind of reception— ecumenical reception.

Quite early in this process, Jean-Marie Tillard, the Dominican scholar, described ecumenical reception as involving a certain danger. If the phrase is used without adequate concern, the expression may become an umbrella term or a catchall. Tillard declared that if this reception means everything, it will finally mean nothing. He discerned already in the 1980s evidence that ecumenical reception was being viewed as reconciliation of a superficial sort. He concluded that the potential ecumenical reception holds for the ecumenical present and future will be lost if it is understood as simply the reestablishment of cordial relations.[8]

While ecumenical reception will inevitably involve documents and the approval of texts by authorities, it must be perceived primarily as a spiritual process. This fact does not make ecumenical reception something vague or abstract. Rather it protects it from being viewed as only a sociological process or a democratic movement looking for a majority vote. The awareness that ecumenical reception operates under the Spirit keeps the churches open to common fidelity to the mind and will of Christ himself.

The definition of ecumenical reception takes on a critical role. Various attempts at such a definition have been made in ecumenical literature.[9] Some years ago, I attempted to survey these efforts.[10] While these attempts differ in detail, an examination discloses that they share much in common. Building on this consensus, I offered a definition that appears to have stood

8. See Tillard, "Reception."

9. Certainly one of the most notable was by Yves Congar. See Congar, "La 'réception' comme réalité ecclésiologique."

10. See Rusch, *Ecumenical Reception*, 58–68.

the test of time. I suggested that ecumenical reception might be thought of as follows:

"[Ecumenical] reception includes all phases and aspects of an ongoing process by which a church under the guidance of God's Spirit makes the results of a bilateral or multilateral conversation a part of its faith and life because the results are seen to be in conformity with the teachings of Christ and of the apostolic community, that is, the gospel as witnessed to in Scripture."[11]

There are obviously differences between classical reception and ecumenical reception, although there are also similarities. Classical reception is mainly associated with the councils of the church and in a period before the rise of the modern ecumenical movement. It included the acceptance of a canon of Scripture, liturgies, prayers, and formulations of doctrine, all of which were viewed as enriching the entire church—a church seen for all its variation as a united church, where the bishop and the local community played key roles.

The context of ecumenical reception is not one united church. Instead there are divided churches that are called to receive from one another. In this setting what is sought is not simply agreement in doctrine but mutual ecclesial reception. This concern raises questions about the continuity of individual churches with the past, about the identification of appropriate organs within these bodies for reception, and about how reception is possible within an incomplete or broken eucharistic community. In ecumenical reception churches for the first time are being asked to receive materials they did not themselves directly and solely produce. This reception involves a fundamental sharing in the one apostolic faith as it has been handed down in many ecclesial communities. Since the 1970s, these church-communities have been struggling to reinterpret their common heritage with new language, new emphases, and new insights—all acquired by participation in the one ecumenical movement.

Some thirty-seven years ago speaking at the meeting of the Commission on Faith and Order in Lima, Peru during the time of

---

11. Rusch, *Ecumenical Reception*, 61.

the exploration of ecumenical reception of *Baptism, Eucharist and Ministry,* Dom Emmanuel Lane stated, "It is also essential that all churches see their reception of this document [*Baptism, Eucharist and Ministry*] concerns them at the very center of being. What is at stake here is the full communion which they desire to recover and the visible unity to which they are called."[12] The challenge of ecumenical reception could not have been put more sharply.

It is helpful to see ecumenical reception as a comprehensive approach and not only as a receiving of ecumenical documents. The final aim of ecumenical reception is not to receive or ratify documents but rather to realize and manifest visible unity between the churches. In a profound sense, this reception begins in an atmosphere of trust even before the establishment of a dialogue and continues on after the dialogue makes its report, and its work is evaluated by the churches. Ecumenical reception should be concerned with the dialogue event as a whole, and not only final texts from a dialogue. The official response of church organs and leaders to a text, and the use of such a text within each church are only parts of a broader reception process.[13]

There is no question that ecumenical reception was not only novel to the ecumenical movement but presented special difficulties. The series of questions at the outset of this chapter illustrates this fact. In addition to such questions there is the basic ecumenical query: what should the desired visible unity of the church look like after centuries of visible disunity? The neglect—neither rejection nor acceptance—of the results of bilateral theological dialogue by sponsoring churches or church organizations is from a certain perspective quite understandable.

Nevertheless, since the churches in the ecumenical movement have committed themselves to such dialogues, even in these difficult circumstances, there are three tasks of ecumenical reception to which they are obligated to give attention.[14]

12. Quoted in Kinnamon, ed., *Towards Visible Unity,* 53.
13. Rusch, *Ecumenical Reception,* 72–77.
14. Rusch, *Ecumenical Reception,* 77–79.

There is, first of all, *reception* in the narrow sense. When representatives the churches have deputed to ecumenical dialogue have found consensus and/or convergence, the *churches* need to respond to these claims of ecclesial consensus and/or convergence. If a church concludes that a particular ecumenical teaching is indeed a faithful witness to the gospel, it must be willing to make it not only formally but also realistically and practically a part of its faith and life, even if the teaching speaks in an accent strange to that church's tradition.

The second task of ecumenical reception could be called non-reception. What is referred to here is the reconsideration and rejection by the *churches* of those portions of their faith and life that obscure or distort the gospel as it has been understood and proclaimed through the centuries. Every tradition has is peculiarities, many of which arose in moments of polemic and heated disagreement. Although they originally may have been a part of the clear identification of gospel, in a new time and context such teachings often obstruct the gospel.

The third task of ecumenical reception may not sound like reception, although it is. This is the process of de-reception. The difference between non-reception and de-reception may seem artificial, but a distinction does exist. It lies in the possibility of differentiating between beliefs and practices in the individual traditions that obscure or distort the gospel (this is what non-reception aims to remove), and beliefs and practices that, although the gospel is not at stake, hinder the visible unity of the church. This is what de-reception aims to remove.

These comments about *non-reception* and *de-reception* should not lead to the conclusion that ecumenical reception requires complete uniformity among the divided churches. Diversity will certainly be an element in any final model, or models, of visible church unity. This diversity will be caused in part by the churches selecting not to non-receive and de-receive certain characteristics of their traditions. This in itself should not be a hindrance to greater unity if what is retained is recognized as appropriate to the life of a specific church, and if other churches can agree that this practice is not contrary to the gospel. This view also acknowledges a certain hierarchy of importance in church teachings. Agreements in areas of a higher priority, e.g., doctrines of the Trinity and Christology, are more significant for ecumenical reception than non-reception and de-reception in other areas.

An additional issue in a chapter dealing with ecumenical reception is the relation of such reception to recognition. Most simply put: which comes first? Do the churches first recognize each other and then receive results of dialogue, or do churches by the act of ecumenical reception recognize each other as churches even if the full meaning of that recognition requires fuller exploration?[15]

There is no question about the intimate relation between these two concepts. No doubt reflection on this topic should continue, yet I would hold to a position that I have developed earlier, viz., that ecumenical reception when successful should result in recognition. If divided churches are able to receive the positive conclusions of their dialogues with other churches, then these churches should be able to move to recognize those other churches as *church*. At that point they should be able to embark on a process aimed at full communion with them, although some aspects of their ecclesiology and doctrine are perhaps not reconciled.[16] It must be acknowledged that such a process could extend over a significant period of time.

This chapter should not conclude with the impression that ecumenical reception is an idea that exists in the abstract but not in reality. Although the full visible unity of divided churches does not yet exist, there are examples of ecumenical reception that demonstrate that such reception has moved some separated churches closer together and nearer that ultimate goal.

For example, the very act of participation in the ecumenical movement is a stage of ecumenical reception. Such an act is

15. For a more adequate review of recognition in ecumenical theology, see Rusch, *Ecumenical Reception*, 81–88.

16. See Rusch, *Ecumenical Reception*, 86–88; Rusch, "'Recognition' as an Ecumenical Concept in the Lutheran-Episcopal Dialogue"; and Kelly, *Recognition*.

recognition in the churches involved that they receive the goal of the ecumenical movement as a visible unity of churches that are now divided.

Membership in local, regional, national, and international councils of churches is a concrete commitment to church unity in spite of all the possible limitations and weaknesses that can be part of such membership. This membership and involvement may be viewed as a form of preliminary ecumenical reception. Often such conciliar memberships result in changes in liturgies, theological education, and cooperative work for social justice. These changes also disclose that ecumenical reception is occurring.

Some specific agreements between divided churches or traditions are further examples of ecumenical reception. These would include the *Leuenberg Agreement* of 1974 between European Lutheran and Reformed churches. This agreement later was extended to non-European churches such as the United Evangelical Lutheran Church of Argentina in 1986. Also to be included is the Covenant of Mission and Faith between the United Church of Christ in the United States and the Evangelical Church of the Union of the former German Democratic Republic and the Federal Republic of Germany in 1981. The *Meissen Agreement* between the Church of England, the Federation of the Evangelical Churches in the German Democratic Republic, and the Evangelical Church in Germany was developed between 1985 and 1988.

Alongside these international instances, there are examples in the United States. The work and progress of the Consultation on Church Union begun in 1961 is an example of steps toward ecumenical reception by its member churches. In 1985 the United Church of Christ and the Christian Church (Disciples of Christ) entered into a partnership that may be considered an example of partial ecumenical reception.

The Evangelical Lutheran Church in America based on commitments made in 1989 in its policy statement, *Ecumenism: The Vision of the Evangelical Lutheran Church in America,* has over the last twenty-some years entered into formal, juridically enacted relationships with several churches.[17] These relations may certainly be regarded as examples of partial ecumenical reception. They either establish relations that may be described as "full communion" or they commit the Evangelical Lutheran Church in America and its partner churches to enter into a process that will culminate in a relation of full communion.[18] These agreements involve the Evangelical Lutheran Church in America in 1997 with the Presbyterian Church (USA), the Reformed Church in America, and the United Church of Christ with a document entitled *Formula of Agreement*, in 1999 with the Episcopal Church with a document entitled *Called to Common Mission*, with the Moravian Church (the Northern and Southern Provinces) with a document entitled *Following Our Shepherd to Full Communion*, and in 2009 with the United Methodist Church with a document entitled *Confessing Our Faith Together*.[19]

A conspicuous feature of the agreements of ecumenical reception, or commitments to it, is that they are inter-Protestant. This fact illustrates that ecumenical reception is easier when there are common bases in culture, history, and theology. Yet the conclusion should not be drawn from this fact that ecumenical reception is impossible outside a pan-Protestant framework. For ecumenical reception to function on a broader scene another concept must be brought into play. To that we turn.

17. See *Ecumenism*.

18. Regarding "full communion," see *Ecumenism*, 27–29.

19. For a fuller description of these relations, see Rusch, *Ecumenical Reception*, 109–16, and www.elca.org/Faith/Ecumenical-and-Inter-Religious-Relations/Full-Communion#.

6

A Recent Ecumenical Concept

Slowness to act officially on the results of the bilateral dialogues has been caused not only by problems associated with ecumenical reception. There has also been the challenge of dealing both with the agreements identified in the dialogues and also with the differences between the churches that persisted through the dialogue process. Clearly the dialogues did not seek uniformity. They held that uniformity was neither desired nor necessary for the visible unity of the church. Here they were in harmony with a long-held view in the ecumenical movement. But how does one evaluate the agreements reached and the remaining differences in terms of the goal of the visible unity of the church? Are the agreements sufficient for church unity? Do the differences preclude expressions of unity? Some differences are clearly reconcilable; others at first glance appear to defy easy rapprochement. Thus, the theological dialogues from the beginning had to confront the relationship and character of difference and consensus.[1]

To understand the issues involved in this discussion, it is useful to look briefly at the early history of twentieth-century ecumenical efforts. This period was characterized by two features: first, multilateral conversations including several churches or traditions, often under the auspices of the Faith and Order Commission, and

1. Invaluable for the topic of this chapter is Wagner, ed., *Einheit—über Wie?* and esp. Meyer, "Die Prägung einer Formel Ursprung und Intention," 36–58; see also Rusch, *Ecumenical Reception,* 118–30.

second, a recognized or assumed vision of church unity best described as organic union. In this model of unity churches were to lose their individual confessional identities in the formation of one new church. Confessional identity and ecumenism were seen to be in tension, if not in hostility.

As mentioned in an earlier chapter, this phase of the ecumenical movement ended in the 1960s with the Second Vatican Council and the entry of the Roman Catholic Church into the one ecumenical movement. There was now a shift of emphasis from multilateral conversations to bilateral dialogues. This transition called into question the necessity of incongruence between confessional identity and ecumenism with its goal of the visible unity of the church. The bilateral dialogues offered a new way to view the relationship between these two commitments. In the initial phases of their work the dialogues performed this task almost unconsciously without formally reflecting on the fact that they were embarking on a novel approach to the search for church unity.

These early dialogues were aware of the "formula of unity" of the New Delhi Assembly of the World Council of Churches, which at least implicitly addressed the issue of unity and diversity.[2] The dialogues grappled with the antagonism between confession (diversity) and ecumenism (unity). Was the only final model for the unity of the church a trans-confessional model? Early on in the dialogues an understanding of unity appeared that provided for overcoming this tension between confession and ecumenism. This new approach allowed both for real unity between the churches and for a legitimate diversity that did not threaten that unity.

Two consultations in 1974 in Geneva formulated the ecumenical theological concept of "unity in reconciled diversity."[3] This idea actually arose quite spontaneously out of the ongoing activity

2. Report of the Section on Unity of the Third Assembly of the World Council of Churches, New Delhi, 1961, 82–84. See also the important discussion of this statement in Meyer, *That All May be One*, 42–7.

3. See Gassmann and Meyer, *The Unity of the Church*, and the Declaration at the sixth assembly of the Lutheran World Federation, *In Christ, A New Community*, 173–75 and 200. See also Meyer, "Einheit in Versöhnter Verschiedenheit."

of the dialogues. In this concept genuine unity was affirmed and the diversities remained without challenging the unity. Such diversities no longer had a church-dividing character. This view of the unity of the church originated in the context of Lutheran dialogue activity, but it was not limited to bilateral dialogues involving Lutherans. It can be found in Anglican-Catholic dialogue, the early reports of the Lutheran-Roman Catholic international dialogue, and for the first time explicitly in the Lutheran-Reformed *Leuenberg Agreement* of 1973.

The *Leuenberg Agreement* originally involved Lutherans, Reformed, and United churches in Germany. The methodology of the document is revealed in the declared recognition of common elements in the churches of the Reformation. The *Agreement* also notes the changed elements in the contemporary situation. It then moves on to an articulation of a discovered consensus in the gospel that includes justification, preaching, baptism, the Lord's Supper, and Christology. Within these aspects of the gospel, it is acknowledged that differences remain between the Lutheran and Reformed traditions. These differences, however, because of the discovered consensus are no longer an obstacle to church fellowship. It is clear that the methodology of the text is: fundamental consensus with differences not challenging that consensus. At the same time the *Agreement* affirms that the condemnations of the sixteenth century are not irrelevant.[4]

As the dialogues proceeded with their work, they began to express their understanding of church unity or church fellowship in a way marked by a reconciliation of doctrines and an overcoming of church-dividing features. Initially they did this without the development of specific formulations. Both the Lutheran-Roman Catholic dialogue and the Anglican-Roman Catholic dialogue spoke of "consensus" or "agreement." They often employed the qualification "a far-reaching consensus" or a "growing consensus."[5] The problem became one of the interpretations given to such expressions. Did they intend to mean that the required consensus

4. See "*Leuenberg Agreement*," especially Sections 1–3, 66–70.
5. See Meyer, "Die Prägung einer Formel," 41–42.

for unity had yet to be reached, and thus further work must be accomplished? Or did they mean that the required understanding for unity had been attained?

The dialogues were struggling, whether consciously or not, to avoid two approaches to doctrinal consensus. One approach would mean that church A would convince church B that church A's position was correct, which would mean that church B's view was in error. The solution would be that church B would convert to the view of church A. There is no real evidence in the dialogue literature that this approach was ever proposed, let alone adopted.

The second approach would involve churches A and B attempting to move out of present doctrinal disagreement by merging their different doctrines into a new synthesis. Here again there is no evidence that this extremely difficult method was ever successful in a dialogue.

The dialogues chose to pursue a different approach. They sought a fellowship between churches of differing confessional stances, where the force of the confessions remains, but where there is respect and allowance for difference. The dialogues found that this could be done by examining the theological concern behind the doctrine. Harding Meyer demonstrated this practice by analyzing the conclusions of the Lutheran-Roman Catholic dialogue on the sacramentality of ordination and the sacrificial character of the Eucharist.[6]

In this process the dialogues were operating on two levels: First, there is a basic agreement of faith. Second there are differences that do remain, but these differences do not call into question the basic agreement of faith. This schema allows space for genuine differences. It is, however, critical to recognize that this model of agreement is not to be viewed as a merely preliminary form of a necessary consensus for unity which requires further development or improvement. This model is not a compromise between two views. It takes the truth claims of each church seriously. It would be a misunderstanding to see the "remaining differences" as something to be endured painfully. Rather, the differences are

6. Meyer, "Die Prägung einer Formel," 44-47.

affirmed because the dialogue has demonstrated that the different confessions do allow these differences. It is surprising to note that the dialogues never actually reflected on or commented on the approach they had in fact adopted.

It should be pointed out that this twofold distinction in levels of agreement—basic agreement in faith and "remaining differences"—is found in the documents of the Second Vatican Council where, for example, in the Decree on Ecumenism reference is made both to diversity in customs and observances, and to legitimate variety in theological expressions of doctrine.[7]

While the description of this model of church unity brought considerable clarification, the problem remained of the exact meaning of terms like "far-reaching consensus" and "growing consensus." Some further refinement was obviously required. Already in the early 1980s there is evidence in ecumenical literature of attempts to find more precise terminology and description for this model of church unity. One resource, among several, was Karl Rahner, who spoke of a "differentiated unity of faith."[8] In 1985 Harding Meyer, in reporting on the second phase of the international Lutheran-Roman Catholic dialogue, described the concept as "differentiated consensus" (*differenzierter Konsens*).[9] Meyer saw this concept of differentiated consensus as overcoming the ambiguity of the idea of "basic consensus." For, as has been explained above, it was precisely differentiated consensus that provided for basic agreement on one level and permitted differences on the other level, while remaining a model for complete church unity.

As the process for the drafting of the *Joint Declaration on the Doctrine of Justification* between Lutherans and Roman Catholics began, Meyer returned to this topic and urged that the proposed declaration on justification be drafted in the framework of differentiated consensus.[10] He saw this approach as being present in the Lutheran-Roman Catholic dialogue from the beginning, as early as

7. See *Unitatis redintegratio*, 16 and 17.

8. See the discussion in Rahner, "Is Church Union Dogmatically Possible?"

9. See Meyer, "Konsens und Kirchengemeinschaft," 182–83.

10. See Meyer, "Ecumenical Consensus."

the *Malta Report* of 1972 with its statements on justification, even if the expression "differentiated consensus" was not present.

The result of these efforts is that the *Joint Declaration on the Doctrine of Justification* is one of the clearest examples of "differentiated consensus." In paragraph 40, the churches of the Lutheran World Federation and the Roman Catholic Church state together that a consensus in the basic truths of the doctrine of justification exists between Lutherans and Roman Catholics.[11] This consensus makes possible two statements in paragraph 41. The first is that the teachings of the Lutheran churches presented in the Declaration do not fall under the condemnations of the Council of Trent. Second, the condemnations in the Lutheran Confessions do not apply to the teachings of the Roman Catholic Church presented in this Declaration.[12] These conclusions are possible because in paragraph 15 the core statement of the text is given, "By grace alone, in faith in Christ's saving work and not because of any merit on our part, we are accepted by God and receive the Holy Spirit, who renews our hearts while equipping and calling us to good works."[13] Yet within this context of consensus, there is both a recognition and appreciation of the remaining differences. This is because the differences do not endanger the fundamental consensus.

This constant pattern in the *Declaration* is a clear example of the use of the concept of "differentiated consensus." The pattern of two levels, one of fundamental agreement on a specific topic, and a second of differences that do not *challenge* this fundamental agreement is evident. The new relation established between the churches of the Lutheran World Federation and the Roman Catholic Church is anchored in a document that seeks ecumenical progress on the basis of "differentiated consensus."

A few years after the signing of the *Joint Declaration on the Doctrine of Justification,* Theodor Dieter, a professor at the Institution for Ecumenical Research in Strasbourg, France, argued that "differentiated consensus" should no longer be considered a

11. See *The Joint Declaration on the Doctrine of Justification,* 25–26.
12. *The Joint Declaration on the Doctrine of Justification,* 26.
13. *The Joint Declaration on the Doctrine of Justification,* 15.

theory but a concept that has ecumenical acceptance. He concluded that this concept and its adoption in the *Joint Declaration on
the Doctrine of Justification* have implications for all the churches
in the ecumenical movement that are yet to be realized.[14] In 2006
the Roman Catholic theologian, Hervé Legrand, expressed his approval of "differentiated consensus" as an ecumenical method to
be pursued.[15] Peter De Mey in 2018 defended the concept as an
invaluable resource for Roman Catholic ecumenism.[16]

Thus the enfolding history of the formulation, "differentiated
consensus," arising in the process of bilateral inter-confessional
dialogues after the Second Vatican Council, has disclosed the dis-
covery of a specific understanding of the unity of the church. This
concept at present has unrealized potential for all the churches in
the ecumenical movement.[17]

This history also revealed that the early identification, discussion, and development of the concept were conducted in German.
This is not surprising since Harding Meyer of the Lutheran World
Federation-related Institute of Ecumenical Research at Strasbourg
has been the major figure in the identification of the idea and the
application of a specific German phrase to describe it. The English
phrase, "differentiated consensus" is a translation of the German,
"differenzierter Konsens."

The German expression has led to further discussion of this
model of unity. Theodor Dieter in 2009 already raised the question
of whether the intention of "differentiated consensus" could better

14. See Dieter, "Die Folgen der Gemeiner Erklärung zur Recht aus evangelischer Sicht."

15. See Legrand, OP, "Receptive Ecumenism and the Future of Ecumenical
Dialogues."

16. See De Mey, "Die Hermeneutik des differenzierten/differenzierenden
Konsenses."

17. To cite just a few examples to date where "differentiated consensus" has
been employed usually without the expressed use of the phrase, see *Leuenberg
Agreement* as it has been described in this chapter. *The Porvoo Common Statement* between Anglicans and Lutherans in Europe, which established a new
relationship between them, implicitly employs the method of differentiated
consensus. See *Together in Mission and Ministry*, 7–15; and Rusch, *Ecumenical
Reception*, 122–23.

be articulated by the phrase a "differentiating consensus." The difference in German is between "differenzierter Konsens" and "differenzierender Konsens." He wrote, "the consensus which is asserted is thus, as one says, a 'differentiated consensus'—one better could say a 'differentiating consensus', which differentiates between that which is held in common, and that in which there clearly can be differences" (translation here).[18] Dieter pursued the same argument in an article as recently as 2015.[19] An important point in this article that is not to be overlooked, and has implications for the subsequent chapter in this book, is that "differentiating consensus" (thus "differentiated consensus") has an ecumenical potential for overcoming not only doctrinal differences between the churches but also differences in ministry and structures.

This latter possibility was clear to me in the preparation of my work on ecumenical reception. Rather than placing the implications for structure under the concept of either a differentiating or a differentiated consensus, I followed the suggestion of Harding Meyer and spoke of a "differentiated participation," in which there is a basic level of agreement about a structure of the church and what participation in such an office or structure would mean. There is also a second level of difference in such participation, which, as in differentiating consensus, would not challenge the first level of agreement.[20]

The distinction between "differentiated" and "differentiating" is presumably more significant in German than in English. Yet in English texts it does raise the question of which term

18. See Dieter, "Zehn Jahre 'Gemeinsame Erklärung zur Rechtfertigungslehre,'"162–74, esp. 164, which reads "der Konsens, der behauptet wird, ist also ein, wie man sagt, 'differenzierter Konsens'—besser würde man von einem differenzierenden Konsens sprechen, also einem Konsens, der differenziert zwischen dem, was gemeinsam ist, und dem worin durchaus Unterschiede sein könnten."

19. See Dieter, "Zu einigen Problemen ökumenischer Hermeneutik."

20. See Rusch, *Ecumenical Reception,* 130–33 and Meyer, "Evangelische Teilhabe am Episkopat?" 244–56, which appeared in English with the title "Differentiated Participation."

should be employed. There are examples in German of the use of both terms together.[21]

Up to this point in this volume the term "differentiated consensus" has been used as an accurate translation of the texts discussed. In the remainder of this work, "differentiating consensus" will be employed. This shift recognizes the discussion that has taken place in the years since the signing of the *Joint Declaration on the Doctrine of Justification*.[22]

---

21. See footnote 16 above.

22. It must be acknowledged that whatever advantages this change in terminology brings, especially for German readers, it does instill in English texts an element of confusion. The International Lutheran-Roman Catholic Commission on Unity published in 2006 a study document entitled *The Apostolicity of the Church*. In §3.6, 292–3 (p. 133) the English text reads in several passages "differentiated consensus." When the German is consulted, the text reads "differenzierender Konsens."

7

A New Type of Ecumenical Document

THE PRECEDING PAGES OF this work have made an overall argument that for an ecumenical advance among the divided churches—i.e., for divided churches to be drawn closer to visible unity—something more is needed than has hitherto been present. This lacuna is in part the absence of ecumenical reception. Acceptance of the results of the bilateral dialogues is required to change the present situation.

For this progression to occur, three things are necessary. First, the churches need to accept the responsibility, occasioned by their involvement in the dialogues, to engage in ecumenical reception. Second, the churches must accept and utilize the concept of differentiating consensus. Third, there must be a vehicle or instrument that allows the churches to affirm authoritatively the differentiating consensus of both agreements and non-church-dividing differences and—extremely importantly—to commit themselves to serious dialogue about unresolved differences in order to determine whether or not they are church-dividing.

This third item will probably take the shape of a declaration. This will be a new type of ecumenical document that has not previously existed. Its distinction will be that it not only includes agreements and non-church-dividing differences, but also indicates differences whose character as church-dividing or not church-dividing have yet to be determined. The exploration of this kind of text will be the focus of this chapter. A specific text will be shared as an example of what is possible.

While the text of this type of document will be something novel in respect to present ecumenical literature and proposals, it is not without forerunners. Three relevant ecumenical texts are described here. These descriptions are not intended to be exhaustive of the existing documents, whose purpose is to affect formal relations among churches.[1] Rather, these accounts will reveal by comparison the distinctiveness that is characteristic of the new genre of document.

The *Leuenberg Agreement*, mentioned in an earlier chapter, came into effect on October 1, 1974.[2] It originally involved the Lutheran, Reformed, and United Churches in Germany. Since 1974 more than 100 European and South American Protestant churches have signed this agreement. The *Leuenberg Agreement* employs the concept of differentiating consensus and identifies two levels of agreement. The text is cognizant of the contemporary situations of the churches. It is clear that it is not a new confession of faith; it does not replace the sixteenth-century confessions. It does declare that a number of the condemnations of the sixteenth century were not necessarily wrong, but they do not apply to the present churches. The document encourages continuing theological discussion among the involved churches, but this conversation does not have as its purpose church fellowship, for by signing the *Agreement* the churches indicate that they are already in fellowship.[3]

1. One could also examine the declarations and texts by which the Evangelical Lutheran Church in America entered into the process leading to "full communion" with six other churches. These relations are all with churches tracing their origins to the sixteenth-century Reformation. The agreements have as their purpose to allow the churches to reach full visible unity, although not organic union. See www.elca.org/Faith/Ecumenical-and-Inter-Religious/Full-Communion# .

2. Regarding the *Leuenberg Agreement*, see Rusch and Martensen, eds., *The Leuenberg Agreement and Lutheran-Reformed Relationships*; and Rusch, "*Leuenberg Agreement*," 245–47.

3. See the *Leuenberg Agreement* in Andrews and Burgess, eds., *An Invitation to Action*, 65. The *Leuenberg Agreement* in "B. Agreement between Reformation Churches in Europe," §1, states "This common understanding of

The second example is the *Porvoo Common Statement* which was approved by various church synods in the years 1994 and 1995. This text is the foundation of church unity between the British and Irish Anglican churches, and the Lutheran churches of Norway, Sweden, Denmark, Iceland, Finland, Estonia, and Lithuania. The Lutheran church of Latvia has an observer-status within the Porvoo relationship. The final chapter of the *Porvoo Common Statement* is a short text with the title "The Porvoo Declaration." The churches together issued this document in which they acknowledge one another's doctrinal basis and ordained ministry. The Declaration reflects the concerns of both sides in this agreement. The Anglican issue was the question of the historic succession of bishops in these Lutheran churches; the Lutheran concern was one of theological confession. The sections on the gospel, baptism, and the Lord's Supper were reassuring to Lutherans. Anglicans accepted the view that these Lutheran churches had kept a ministry of oversight (*episcope*) and that historic episcopal succession was a "sign" that does not alone guarantee every aspect of the apostolic faith. Without the use of the term, differentiating consensus, it is possible to see the concept as present in the *Porvoo Common Statement* and Declaration. The text of the latter makes clear that the signing churches now view themselves in a new and closer relation of unity.[4]

The final document to be mentioned in this context is the *Joint Declaration on the Doctrine of Justification* between the Lutheran churches of the Lutheran World Federation and the Roman Catholic Church. This text has been mentioned several times in the preceding chapters. It is noteworthy because to date it is the only report based on the Lutheran-Roman Catholic dialogue to receive official action by the sponsoring bodies. It is also a clear example of how differentiating consensus can resolve a

---

the gospel enables them [the signing churches] to *declare* and *realize* church fellowship," (66, ital. here).

4. See Saarinen, "Porvoo Common Statement"; and *Together in Mission and Ministry*, "The Porvoo Declaration," 30–31. Of considerable interest in this connection is also Tjørhom, ed., *Apostolicity and Unity*.

doctrinal dispute between churches of the Reformation and the Roman Catholic Church.

The *Joint Declaration on the Doctrine of Justification* illustrates several significant points.[5] Unlike intra-Protestant declarations that can lead to expressions of full visible unity between churches, this text resolves the church-dividing character of only one doctrine that divides Lutherans and Roman Catholics. This is admittedly a critical church teaching in Lutheran-Roman Catholic relations, but not the only one. The *Declaration* has created good will and made a number of cooperative efforts between Lutherans and Roman Catholics possible. It has provided a test case of how to address other divisive issues. Yet it has not altered the official relationship between the Roman Catholic Church and the Lutheran churches.

In this respect it differs most sharply from the *Leuenberg Agreement* and the *Porvoo Common Statement*. The conclusion becomes clear that in terms of Lutheran-Roman Catholic relations and in general, Protestant church relations with Catholicism and Orthodoxy, another type of ecumenical text is needed. Such a text would do what these mentioned texts have not been able to accomplish. It would, first, by means of differentiating consensus identify fundamental, common areas of agreement. It would, second, identify differences that do not challenge this fundamental, common consensus. And third, it would identify differences that may or may not be church-dividing, but require further exploration.

Such a document would provide a means for churches to take *official and juridical action* that would claim a differentiating consensus on certain aspects of topics like church, ministry, and the Eucharist. The new type of text would also call for *substantial, official, and juridical action* in regard to the unresolved issues. This would be a new feature. The value of this new kind of text would be that on the official level *the churches would own certain conclusions of the dialogues* so that those topics would never need to be revisited to determine if they are church-dividing. The document would also

---

5. See also the discussion of *The Joint Declaration on the Doctrine of Justification* and references in chapter 6.

help determine the future course of dialogues by identifying those topics or aspects of this topic that need further exploration.

This component, i.e., juridical action by the churches taking part in ecumenical dialogues, is the critical element in this new type of ecumenical document. Its adoption officially would not lead the churches that signed it into full visible unity, but such a juridical reception would be an important step in that direction and demonstrate that ecumenical initiative has not been lost.

In the light of the new context caused by the creation and reception of such a document, the *churches* could explore together what difference this *official and juridical action* makes for the actual lived relations between divided churches. This would be particularly true if the topics addressed in such a text were church, ministry, and the Eucharist. The issues involved here will become clearer if one bilateral dialogue, and its relationships, is employed as an example. It must also be emphasized that what is said here about one bilateral dialogue and its relationships could have direct implications for other such dialogues and relationships.

The immediate challenge to be faced is that such a genre of ecumenical literature has not thus far existed in any dialogue. In 2003 and 2005 Harding Meyer published two articles proposing the creation of this kind of document in the Lutheran-Roman Catholic context especially on the topic of the Eucharist.[6] In the article published in 2003, Meyer actually outlined what a text of such a statement or declaration should contain.

Using the concept of a differentiating consensus, he illustrated both the agreements and differences that remain in regard both to Christ's eucharistic presence, and the Eucharist as sacrifice. He also drew attention to some practical and pastoral aspects of the sacrament. The document envisioned by Meyer would thus acknowledge the fundamental consensus between Lutherans and Roman Catholics about the Eucharist, the non-church-dividing differences, and

---

6. See Meyer, ". . . 'genuinam atque integram substantiam Mysterii eucharistici non servasse . . .' ," and "Der Sich Abzeichnende Evangelische/ Katholische Konsens im Theologischen Verständnis des Euchariste und die Frage der Euchariste-Gemeinschaft," 165–82 and esp. 180.

areas where further work must be done. The purpose of such a text would be to assure the consensus reached and to secure a commitment to address the continuing differences. These characteristics soon lead to the idea of a "*document in via.*" Its lack of total agreement on the topic should not render it less important.

In 2010 Gunther Wenz published an article based on an earlier presentation he made to the International Lutheran-Roman Catholic Commission on Christian Unity.[7] The article recognizes its debt to the earlier work of Harding Meyer and supports the idea of the feasibility and appropriateness of a joint Lutheran-Roman Catholic declaration on the Eucharist. Using the ideas contained in differentiating consensus, Wenz both points to commonalities in Eucharistic teachings and notes differences between Lutherans and Catholics regarding the sacrament. These differences in many cases do not exclude each other. Wenz argues that the issues of church fellowship and eucharistic fellowship belong together. They do need to be distinguished, but they should not be separated.

Two years later in 2012 the journal *Ökumenische Rundschau* published two articles on the theme of a joint declaration on the Lord's Supper, one by a Roman Catholic theologian, Dorothea Sattler, and the other by a Lutheran theologian, Friederike Nüssel.[8] Both articles agree that the subject is one that merits consideration. Nüssel is somewhat more hopeful about the realization of such a project, but both theologians raise a critical question about what is the practical result of such a text when important and interrelated questions about church, its apostolicity, and ministry are not addressed. Both authors recognize that the dialogue over the years has resolved many points, and raise the question: could a declaration on the Eucharist be a preliminary step to addressing these other topics?

---

7. See Wenz, "Skizze des Entwurfs einer Gemeinsamen Erklärung zur Lehre vom Herrenmahl."

8. See Sattler, "Auf dem Weg zu einer 'Gemeinsamen Erklärung zum Herrenmahl'?"; and Nüssel, "Ist eine 'Gemeinsame Erklärung zum Herrenmahl' möglich und sinnvoll?"

These discussions, largely on the Lutheran side, have much in common with the efforts and statements of such Roman Catholics as Cardinal Walter Kasper in 2009 and Cardinal Kurt Koch in 2011, the former and present Presidents of the Pontifical Council for Promoting Christian Unity.[9] This seems also true of the ecumenical stance of Pope Francis.[10]

All these factors point to a context where it is fitting to attempt to create a new genre of ecumenical text. This text uses differentiating consensus to recognize fundamental agreements, and also employs differentiating consensus to explore remaining differences, and finally makes a commitment to continuing dialogue to address these differences. The purpose of such a text is to enable the sponsoring churches in an appropriate manner to take substantial, official, and juridical action that would advance them together toward the goal of common mission and the visible unity of Christ's church. This situation exists in a number of bilateral relations. Because of its history and promise the Lutheran-Roman Catholic is an appropriate test case.

What follows is an attempt by this author to imagine such a text. What is here offered enjoys no authority beyond its intrinsic content. It is an amendable text to which improvement can be offered. This text should be seen as a contribution to further steps toward visible unity and the mission of Christ's church not only by Lutherans and Roman Catholics, but also by others in the ecumenical movement.[11]

9. See, e.g., Kasper, *Harvesting the Fruits*, and Koch, "Il Pontifico Consiglio per la Promozione dell' Unita dei Cristiani Sviluppi e efide dell'ecumenismo."

10. See Destivelle, "Le Pape Francois et l'Unite des Chretiens;" Pope Francis, *Evangelii Gaudium*; and Braüer, "Pope Francis and Ecumenism."

11. It will become apparent in the reading and studying of the following text there is an indebtedness to an earlier ecumenical document. In 2015 the United States Conference of Catholic Bishops through its Committee on Ecumenical and Interreligious Affairs and the Evangelical Lutheran Church in America through its Office of the Presiding Bishop published a text entitled *Declaration on the Way*. This document is a significant ecumenical text that merits careful attention and study. What the *Declaration on the Way* cannot do because of its length, structure, and type of recommendations is be a vehicle for the essential feature of any declaration in via, viz., the *substantial, official,*

A Possible Declaration *In Via:*
On Church, Eucharist, and Ministry

Agreements on the Church

Roman Catholics and Lutherans confess and recognize together that the church of Jesus Christ:

- Has been assembled as the body and bride of Christ by the Triune God, who grants its members a sharing in the Triune divine life as God's own people.

- Is gathered by the proclamation of the gospel of God's saving mercy in Christ, proclaimed in the Holy Spirit by the apostles.

- Lives from and is ruled by the Word of God which it encounters in Christ.

- Participates in Christ's benefits through the proclaiming of the gospel, the practice of baptism as the basis of Christian fellowship, and the celebration of the Eucharist which promotes and strengthens this fellowship.

- Acknowledges these sacraments as initiated by Christ and handed on by his apostles.

- Is a communion *(koinonia)* sharing God's gifts offered by Christ and held in a unity and fellowship of believers.

- Is indefectible, being preserved by the Holy Spirit in all aspects essential for salvation.

- Is mandated on earth to carry out its mission, as an essential characteristic of its being, in which it participates in God's activity in the world by evangelization, worship, service to humanity, and care of creation.

---

and juridical reception of the dialogues' findings by the sponsoring churches. For one negative critique among several of *Declaration on the Way* see Rusch, "Declaration on the Way."

Therefore, Catholics and Lutherans are able to confess and recognize together that in each other's ecclesial communities the church of Jesus Christ is present (cf. 1 Cor 1:2; 2 Cor 1:1).

> *The above statements indicate that Roman Catholics and Lutherans affirm the ecclesial character of each other's communities. These affirmations provide a basis for a process to explore the mutual recognition of ordained ministry, given by God's grace to Lutherans and Roman Catholics.*

Agreements on the Ordained Ministry

Roman Catholics and Lutherans confess and recognize together that in their ecclesial communities they acknowledge an ordained ministry that:

- Contributes through the power of the Holy Spirit to the church's continuing apostolic faithfulness.
- Is transmitted by the laying on of hands and prayer as an unrepeatable action (ordination).
- Enhances the common priesthood of all the baptized, which likewise enriches the ordained ministry.
- Has as foremost among its various tasks the proclamation of the gospel.
- Has the essential and specific function of assembling and building up of the Christian community by proclaiming God's word and celebrating the sacraments.
- Has a divine commission to serve in the community and for the community.
- Has authority within and over the community.
- Is one ordained ministerial office, containing within it a special ministry of *episcope* as a form of service in the proclamation of the Word and in correct teaching as regards presbyters/pastors.
- Serves the unity of the worldwide church.

The above consensus on the church and ministry furnish the context for agreements about the Eucharist (the Lord's Supper).

Agreements on the Eucharist

Roman Catholics and Lutherans confess and recognize together that they share the following understandings of the Eucharist (Lord's Supper).

- The celebration of the Eucharist is both a great gift and a lasting charge that Jesus Christ bequeathed to his followers on the night of his betrayal.

- The assembly of Christians for this celebration is a witness since apostolic times to this action of Christ.

- In the receiving of Christ's body and blood in the Holy Communion, believers share the spiritual benefits of union with the Risen Christ.

- Through the Lord's Supper the church participates in a unique way in the life of the Trinity.

- In eucharistic worship, there is the memorial *(anamnesis)* that includes not only a subjective remembrance but an objective remembrance of the cross and resurrection of the Lord who is present as the one crucified and risen, to whom the church responds with its sacrifice of praise and thanksgiving.

- In the sacrament of the Lord's Supper Jesus Christ himself is present truly and substantially as a person in his entirety as Son of God and a human being.

- In the eucharistic communion there is a sacramental participation in the glorified body and blood of Christ as a pledge of eternal life in Christ.

- In the sharing in the celebration of the Eucharist, there is an essential sign of the unity of the church.

- In the Lord's Supper, there is a mirror of and building up of the church in its unity.

    The understanding of church, ministry, and Eucharist expressed in the above common confessions and recognitions shows that on these aspects of church, ministry, and Eucharist a substantial consensus exists between Lutherans and Roman Catholics.

The following text is a suggestion for a substantial, official, and juridical action by appropriate Lutheran and Roman Catholic authorities. Exact wording would need to be achieved in close collaboration.

    Therefore by the act of signing this declaration the Lutheran churches (alternative reading: the Lutheran World Federation) and the Roman Catholic Church confirm this substantial consensus on church, ministry, and the Eucharist, and declare that in regard to the enumerated agreements any remaining differences do not destroy this consensus and no longer have a church-dividing character.

Remaining Differences

Differences Regarding the Church

While Lutherans and Roman Catholics have reached substantial consensus on the topic of the church in their dialogues, describing it as "a fellowship of believers" and "people of God," aspects of this subject remain where they hold differing views. These views divide the churches. The question to be answered is whether these differences are of a nature to continue to divide the church.

- One way Roman Catholics have recently described the church is as a "sacrament of salvation." Lutherans have tended not to use this terminology.

- Lutherans and Roman Catholics both have spoken of the church as "holy" and acknowledged the presence of sin in the church. Catholics have refrained from calling the church it-self "sinful." Lutherans have tended to acknowledge that even the institutional form of the church can be involved in sin.

- Lutherans and Roman Catholics agree that the church is authorized by God and empowered by the Holy Spirit to teach and distinguish truth from error. Catholics have acknowledged a special responsibility and authority entrusted to the episcopate. Lutherans have rejected a role of papal authority that places it over Scripture.

- Both Lutherans and Roman Catholics recognize in differing ways the necessary role of the faithful, who share in the witnessing to the apostolic message, in the reception of teaching.

- Roman Catholics hold that individual churches, fellowships gathered around a bishop, are totally the church in communion with other such churches. In these churches the bishop with the clergy are formed into one by the Holy Spirit and eucharistic celebrations. Lutherans hold that the church is present in its essential elements in a congregation of believers in which the gospel is preached and the sacraments are administered in accord with the gospel by rightly called and ordained ministers, some of whom exercise pastoral authority to pastors and a role in opposing false teaching.

Differences Regarding the Ordained Ministry

Lutherans and Roman Catholics have held differing views about ministry for long periods of time. These conflicting positions have not only been present in the sixteenth century, but also new difficulties arose in the course of the nineteenth and twentieth centuries.

- In recent times the first problem to occur was the decision and practice of some Lutheran churches to ordain women to the pastoral office and to provide for the possibility of ordained women filling the episcopal office. The decision and practice has been rejected by the Roman Catholic Church.

- The ecumenical context, especially after *Baptism, Eucharist and Ministry,* offers some hope for a differentiating consensus on some aspects of ministry, and perhaps some possibility for nuanced steps towards mutual recognition and reconciliation.

- Lutherans are able to recognize the apostolic character of Roman Catholic ordained ministry. Roman Catholics recognize in the Lutheran ordained ministry important elements which are essential to the apostolic office. They have spoken of *defectus ordinis" (Unitatis Redintegratio* 22) not to be understood as a complete absence, but rather as a "lack."

- Roman Catholics and Lutherans have characterized one another's position on the common priesthood of the faithful in ways that suggest important differences on this topic. While their confessional documents say otherwise, Lutherans have given at times the impression that there is no difference between the office of the ordained ministry and the priesthood of the baptized, and that the office of the ordained ministry derives its authority from the common priesthood of the faithful. Catholics have expressed the difference between the general and hierarchical priesthood as one of essence and not only degree. Lutherans have tended not to speak in this way.

- Catholics regard ordination as one of the seven sacraments. Lutherans do not generally describe ordination as a sacrament.

- Roman Catholics hold that episcopal consecration confers the fullness of ordination. Lutherans hold that ordained ministry is fully realized in the public service of Word and sacrament in the local community, while recognizing within the one office a role for *episcope* that extends beyond the local community.

- Lutherans and Catholics have disagreed historically about the nature and function of a universal ministry in the church as exercised by the Bishop of Rome. Today Lutherans and Catholics recognize different positions on this subject exist within Catholicism. New convergences between Catholics and Lutherans now are present, and the harsh condemnations of the past are not suitable. For Lutherans questions remain about the nature of the visible unity of the universal church and how this universal church can speak authoritatively.

Differences Regarding the Eucharist

Lutherans and Roman Catholics from the sixteenth century have disagreed about aspects of teaching about the Eucharist (Lord's Supper).

- Lutherans and Roman Catholics historically have disagreed about how *sacrifice* as a term and concept should be applied to the Lord's Supper. Catholic teaching that the Eucharist is neither a new sacrifice, nor a repetition or completion of the once-and-for-all sacrifice on the cross, holds promise of over-coming some of the disagreements on this subject.

- Roman Catholics and Lutherans have employed different theological statements and terminology in regard to the mode of presence of Christ in the Eucharist. Catholics use the term *transubstantiation* as highly appropriate to speak of the mode of presence. Lutherans have in their Confessions rejected this term, although Catholic insistence that this term does not explain the miracle of the real presence holds the promise of possible agreement in the area of terminology.

- Lutherans and Roman Catholics have traditionally disagreed in their view and practice regarding the eucharistic elements after the conclusion of the liturgical celebration. Recently some Lutheran churches have given attention to the reverential use of the remaining bread and wine in ways that address Catholic concern with this matter.

- Roman Catholics and Lutherans have traditionally disagreed about the practice of the adoration of Christ in the eucharistic elements. Catholics practice such adoration; Lutherans do not.

- Lutherans generally invite all baptized believers to receive the Lord's Supper. Catholics generally invite only those in full communion with the Catholic Church, although after the Second Vatican Council a more nuanced position has been taken in many places.

> *The above section contains material on church, ministry, and Eucharist where at the present time Lutheran-Roman Catholic total agreement has not yet been reached. Whether these differences are tolerable in a differentiating consensus so as to allow greater expressions of visible unity remains an open question. This is also true of the question of whether the weight of these differences inhibits fuller unity.*

The following text is a suggestion for *substantial, official, and juridical action* by the appropriate Lutheran and Roman Catholic authorities. Exact wording would need to be achieved by close collaboration.

> *Therefore by the act of signing this declaration the Lutheran churches (alternative reading: the Lutheran World Federation) and the Roman Catholic Church commit themselves to continued dialogue on these matters, praying for the guidance of God's Spirit to lead them into greater visible unity.*

Notes

Agreements on the Church

Report of the Joint Lutheran-Roman Catholic Study Commission on "The Gospel and the Church" ("The Malta Report"), 1972.
Facing Unity. The Lutheran-Roman Catholic Joint Commission, 1984.

Church and Justification (Kirche und Rechtfertigung). The Lutheran-Roman Catholic Joint Commission, 1994.
Apostolicity of the Church: Study Document of the Lutheran-Roman Catholic Commission on Unity, 1996.
Teaching Authority and Infallibility in the Church, Lutherans and Catholics in Dialogue VI, 1978.
Kirchengemeinschaft in Wort und Sakrament, 1994.
Communio Sanctorum: The Church as the Communion of Saints, 2000.
The Church as Koinonia of Salvation: Its Structures and Ministries, 2004.
Justification in the Life of the Church: A Report from the Roman Catholic-Lutheran Dialogue Group for Sweden and Finland, 2010.

Agreements on the Ordained Ministry

Report of the Joint Lutheran-Roman Catholic Study Commission on "The Gospel and the Church" ("The Malta Report"), 1972.
The Ministry in the Church: Roman Catholic-Lutheran Joint Commission, 1981.
Facing Unity: Roman Catholic-Lutheran Joint Commission, 1984.
Eucharist and Ministry, Lutherans and Catholics in Dialogue IV, 1970.

Agreements on the Eucharist

The Eucharist (Das Herrenmahl), Lutheran-Roman Catholic Joint Commission, 1978.
The Eucharist as Sacrifice: Lutherans and Catholics in Dialogue III, 1967.
Kirchengemeinschaft in Wort und Sakrament, 1984.

Differences Regarding the Church

Church and Justification (Kirche und Rechtfertigung) Lutheran-Roman Catholic Joint Commission, 1993.
Apostolicity of the Church: Study Document of the Lutheran-Roman Catholic Commission on Unity, 2006.
Communio Sanctorum: The Church as the Communion of Saints, 2000.
The Church as Koinonia of Salvation: Its Structures and Ministries, 2004.

Differences Regarding the Ordained Ministry

Report of the Joint Lutheran-Roman Catholic Study Commission on "The Gospel and the Church" ("The Malta Report"), 1972.

Papal Primacy and the Universal Church, Lutherans and Catholics in Dialogue V, 1974.
The Ministry in the Church, Roman Catholic-Lutheran Joint Commission, 1981.
The Church as Koinonia of Salvation: Its Structures and Ministries, 2004.
Apostolicity of the Church: Study Document of the Lutheran-Roman Catholic Commission on Unity, 2006.
Justification in the Life of the Church: A Report from the Roman Catholic-Lutheran Dialogue Group for Sweden and Finland, 2010.

Differences Regarding the Eucharist

The Eucharist (Das Herrenmahl), Lutheran-Roman Catholic Commission, 1978.
The Eucharist as Sacrifice: Lutherans and Roman Catholics in Dialogue III, 1967.
Eucharist and Ministry: Lutherans and Catholics in Dialogue IV, 1970.
Justification in the Life of the Church: A Report from the Roman Catholic-Lutheran Dialogue Group for Sweden and Finland, 2010.

8

A Concluding Word

THE TRADITIONAL MARKS OF the church—one, holy, catholic, and apostolic—have never in the history of the church been seen as self-imposed characteristics. Rather they have been understood as a comprehensive vision of the church that comes from Scripture itself. The conviction is that the Lord of the church wishes this community of faith to exhibit these four descriptive markers. Whether churches are creedal or non-creedal, most churches affirm or at least on occasion recite the Nicene (more exactly the Nicene-Constantinopolitan) Creed of AD 381. This creed reflects the scriptural understanding of the Christian community as it calls believers to confess, "We believe in one, holy, catholic, and apostolic church." It is not surprising that this creed can claim in terms of its teaching almost unanimous acceptance by various church bodies throughout history.

Nevertheless, any accurate reading of history reveals how the church has struggled to live out these marks. While this is true for all four of the adjectives, it is particularly valid for the word *one* and the concept of the unity of the church. Obviously, the church of Christ has through the centuries been more disunited than united.

This fact has been actualized, accepted, and shielded by a number of explanations. These rationales include the assertion that only one particular church is truly *the* church. Thus if it is united at least in structure the unity of the church has been maintained. Another defense is the notion that the affirmation of the creed can be understood as a reference to the *invisible unity* of the church. Therefore if the churches are visibly not one, that visible disunity is not necessarily in contradiction to Scripture and the creed.

Another factor in recent years has been a shift of interest within the ecumenical movement itself. The early attention of this multifaceted movement to the unity of the churches has been largely replaced by concerns about other aspects of the movement, such as peace and social justice. These areas are indeed important and worthy of attention, but when unity loses its central place in the movement, the nature of the movement itself changes. This dislocation has occurred at the same time that the churches themselves have become more and more occupied with questions of their own identity and survival. In such a setting to speak of the visible unity of the church can appear to be threatening.

The changing world scene marked by the advance of secularism and an often uncritical acceptance of pluralism runs counter to the notion of and commitment to the visible unity of Christ's church. The early exhilaration of ecumenical hopes immediately after the Second Vatican Council appears to have been unrealistic for many individuals fifty years later.

In spite of all these hindrances, throughout the centuries and in the present, the ecumenical concern for the visible unity of the church has not been lost. This is certainly true in the last hundred years. Indeed, commitment to this vision of unity actually received an added impetus with the Second Vatican Council. The notion that the unity of the church has as its essential presupposition the already-given oneness of the church is alive in ecumenical theology. Simultaneously, there is the recognition that this primary goal of unity is yet to be realized in history. This means the ecumenical task remains the same: to manifest this oneness of the church and to make it visible and effective.

Great efforts and energy, along with the talent and commitment of many unsung women and men, have been expended to see this vision advance. Considerable success has been achieved in the twentieth century. For many this accomplishment has come about through the guidance and assistance of the Holy Spirit. Still, the ultimate goal of the visible unity of Christ's church has proven to be inaccessible. As historic issues causing division have been resolved, fresh concerns have arisen that have the potential to divide the churches on new issues. Clearly, the final attainment of visible church unity will come in the Triune God's good time. Nevertheless, a frustration exists in church bodies and individuals that more has not been achieved in the ecumenical life and witness of the churches, especially in view of the theological success of many dialogues.

The chief argument of this book has been that there are now tools available to the churches to move toward their common future of being one visibly united church. These resources have come out of the ecumenical experience itself. They include an understanding of ecumenical reception, an acceptance of the theological category of differentiating consensus, and the development of documents *in via*, including their juridical and official approval.

Since the heart of this work is a proposal to the churches, and this proposal still stands before the churches, it is impossible to draw final conclusions about the thesis described in the seven previous chapters. The state of Christianity in the opening decades of this century is neither one of confidence nor tranquility. In such a context will even ecumenically committed churches employ the three instruments of ecumenical reception, differentiating consensus, and documents *in via*? If they do, they will be drawn by God's Spirit into a new and unknown future. But it will be a future that more closely than the present mirrors the will of the Lord of the church for his church.

On the eve of the opening of the Second Vatican Council over fifty years ago, Peter Brunner, professor of systematic theology in Heidelberg University, Germany, wrote: "If it is God's will and we have faith, then in this future not only that church will be one which is being built into the body of Jesus Christ through the Word and Sacrament, but also that church which delivers the means of salvation to the world and in this delivery is now divided."[1]

1. Brunner, "The Mystery of the Division and the Unity of the Church," 209.

These words are as true now as they were in 1961. They hold forth the promise given to divided churches of a *common future* together in the full visible unity of the church.

Bibliography

Almen, Lowell G., and Richard J. Sklba, eds. *The Hope of Eternal Life: Lutherans and Catholics in Dialogue XI*. Minneapolis: Lutheran University Press, 2011.

Anderson, H. George, Francis Stafford, and Joseph A. Burgess, eds. *Justification by Faith: Lutherans and Catholics in Dialogue VII*. Minneapolis: Augsburg, 1985.

———. *The One Mediator, the Saints, and Mary: Lutherans and Catholics in Dialogue VIII*. Minneapolis: Augsburg, 1992.

Andrews, James, E. and Joseph A. Burgess, eds. *An Invitation to Action: The Lutheran-Reformed Dialogue, Series III*. Philadelphia: Fortress, 1984.

The Apostolicity of the Church: A Study Document of the Lutheran-Roman Catholic Commission on Unity. Minneapolis: Lutheran University Press, 2006.

Augustine. *Confessions*. Edited by Henry Chadwick. Oxford: Oxford University Press, 1991.

Baptism, Eucharist and Ministry. Faith and Order, Paper 111. Geneva: World Council of Churches, 1982.

Best, Thomas F. "Councils of Churches: Local, National, Regional." In *Dictionary of the Ecumenical Movement*, 2d ed., edited by Nicholas Lossky, José Míguez Bonino, John Pobee, Thomas Stransky, Geoffrey Wainwright, and Pauline Webb, 255–63. Geneva: World Council of Churches, 2002.

Best, Thomas F., Lorelei Fuchs, SA, John Gibaut, Jeffrey Gros, FSC, and Despina Prassas, eds. *Growth in Agreement IV, 1 and 2, 2005–2013*. Geneva: World Council of Churches, 2017.

Bilheimer, Robert S. *Breakthrough: The Emergence of the Ecumenical Tradition*. Grand Rapids: Eerdmans, 1989.

Birmelé, André and Wolfgang Thönissen, eds. *Auf dem Weg zur Gemeinschaft: 50 Jahre international evangelisch-lutherische/römisch-katholischer Dialogue*. Leipzig: Evangelische Verlaganstalt and Paderborn: Bonifatius, 2018.

Bolen, Donald, Nicholas Jesson, and Donna Geernaert, SC, eds. *Towards Unity: Ecumenical Dialogue 500 Years after the Reformation*. New York: Paulist, 2017.

Brandreth, Henry Renaud Turner, OGS. "Approaches of the Churches Towards each Other in the Nineteenth Century." In *A History of the Ecumenical Movement, 1517–1948*, 2d ed., edited by Ruth Rouse and Stephen Charles Neill, 263–306. Philadelphia: Westminster, 1967.

Braüer, Martin. "Pope Francis and Ecumenism." *Ecumenical Review* 69 (March 2017) 4–14.

Briggs, John, Mercy Amba Oduyoye, and Georges Tsetsis, eds. *A History of the Ecumenical Movement*, Vol. 3. Geneva: World Council of Churches, 2004.

Brunner, Peter. "The Mystery of the Division and the Unity of the Church." In *The Papal Council and the Gospel*, edited by Kristen E. Skydsgaard, 170–209. Minneapolis: Augsburg, 1961.

Cassidy, Edward Idris. *Ecumenism and Interreligious Dialogue: Unitatis Redintegratio, Nostra Aetate*. New York: Paulist, 2005.

The Church: Towards a Common Vision. Faith and Order Paper 214. Geneva: World Council of Churches, 2013.

Congar, Yves. "La reception comme réalite ecclesiologique." *Revue des sciences philosophique et théologique* 65 (1972) 500–14.

Constitution of the World Council of Churches. In *God in Your Grace . . . Official Report of the Ninth Assembly of the World Council of Churches*, edited by Luis N. Rivera-Pagán, 448–49. Geneva: WCC Publications, 2007.

Daniélou, Jean. *A History of Early Christian Doctrine Before the Council of Nicaea*, Vol. 1, *The Theology of Jewish Christianity*, London: Darton, Longman, and Todd, 1964; Vol. 2, *The Gospel Message and Hellenistic Culture*, London: Darton, Longman, and Todd, 1973.

Declaration on the Way: Church, Ministry and Eucharist. Washington, DC: Bishops' Committee for Ecumenical and Interreligious Affairs, United States Conference of Catholic Bishops and Chicago: Evangelical Lutheran Church in America, 2015.

De Mey, Peter. "Die Hermeneutik des differenzierten/differerzierenden Konsenses: Einmaliges: Zugeständnis oder breit einsetzbare ökumenische Methode für die römisch-katholische Kirche?" In *Auf dem Weg zur Gemeinschaft: 50 Jahre international evangelisch-lutherische/römisch-katholischer Dialogue*, edited by André Birmelé and Wolfgang Thönissen, 385–403. Leipzig: Evangelische Verlanganstalt and Paderborn: Bonifatius, 2018.

Destivelle, H., "Le Pape Francois et l'Unite des Chretiens." *Istina* LX (2015) 6–40.

Dieter, Theodor. "Die Folgen der Gemeiner Erklärung zur Recht aus evangelischer Sicht." *Una Sancta* 59.2 (2004) 134–44.

———. "Zehn Jahre 'Gemeinsame Erklärung zur Rechtfertigungslehre: Eine Zwischenblanz aus lutherischer Sicht." *Theologie und Glaube* 52 (2009) 162–74.

BIBLIOGRAPHY

———. "Zu einigen Problemen ökumenischer Hermeneutik." *Una Sancta 70* (2015) 163–70.

Dunn, James D. G. *Unity and Diversity in the New Testament*. Philadelphia: Westminster, 1977.

Ecumenism: The Vision of the Evangelical Lutheran Church in America. Minneapolis: Augsburg, 1994.

Ehrenström, Nils. "Movements for International Friendship and Life and Work." In *A History of the Ecumenical Movement, 1517–1948*, 2d ed., edited by Ruth Rouse and Stephen Charles Neill, 545–96. Philadelphia: Westminster, 1967.

Ehrenström, Nils, and Günther Gassmann. *Confessions in Dialogue.* 3rd ed. Geneva: World Council of Churches, 1975

Empie, Paul C., and T. Austin Murphy, eds. *Lutherans and Catholics in Dialogue I–III.* New York: USA National Committee of the Lutheran World Federation and Washington, DC: Bishops' Committee for Ecumenical and Interreligious Affairs, n.d.

———. *Eucharist and Ministry: Lutherans and Catholics in Dialogue IV.* New York: USA National Committee of the Lutheran World Federation and Washington, DC: Bishops' Committee for Ecumenical and Interreligious Affairs, 1970.

———. *Papal Primacy and the Universal Church: Lutherans and Catholics in Dialogue V.* Minneapolis: Augsburg, 1974.

———. *Teaching Authority and Infallibility in the Church: Lutherans and Catholics in Dialogue VI.* Minneapolis: Augsburg, 1978.

Fahlbusch, Erwin, Jan Milič Lochman, John Mbiti, Jaroslav Pelikan, and Lukas Vischer, eds. *The Encyclopedia of Christianity*, Vols. 1–5. Grand Rapids: Eerdmans and Leiden: Brill, 1999–2008.

Fey, Harold E., ed. *A History the Ecumenical Movement: Vol 2, 1948–1968.* Philadelphia: Westminster, 1970.

Forell, George Wolfgang, and James, McCue, eds. *Confessing One Faith: A Joint Commentary on the Augsburg Confession by Lutheran and Catholic Theologians.* Minneapolis: Augsburg, 1982.

Francis. *Evangelii Gaudium.* Vatican City: Editrice Vaticana, 2013.

From Conflict to Communion: Lutheran-Catholic Common Commemoration of the Reformation in 2017. Grand Rapids: Eerdmans, 2017.

Gassmann, Günther. "Faith and Order." In *Dictionary of the Ecumenical Movement*, 2d ed., edited by Nicholas Lossky, José Míguez Bonino, John Pobee, Thomas Stransky, Geoffrey Wainwright, and Pauline Webb, 461–63. Geneva: World Council of Churches, 2002.

Gassmann, Günther, and Harding Meyer. *The Unity of the Church: Requirements and Structures.* Geneva: *Lutheran World Federation Report* 15 (June, 1983).

Gros, Jeffrey, FSC, Thomas F. Best, and Lorelei F. Fuchs, SA, eds. *Growth in Agreement III: International Dialogue Texts and Agreed Statement, 1998–2005.* Grand Rapids: Eerdmans and Geneva: World Council of Churches, 2007.

Gros, Jeffrey, FSC, Harding Meyer, and William G. Rusch, eds. *Growth in Agreement II: Reports and Agreed Statements of Ecumenical Conversations on a World Level, 1982–1998*. Grand Rapids: Eerdmans and Geneva: World Council of Churches, 2000.

Hopkins, Howard. *John Mott, 1865–1955: A Biography*. Grand Rapids: Eerdmans, 1975.

In Christ, A New Community: The Proceedings of the Sixth Assembly of the Lutheran World Federation, Dar es Salaam, Tanzania, June 13–25, 1977. Geneva: The Lutheran World Federation, 1977.

Irvin, Dale T., and Scott W. Sunquist. *History of the World Christian Movement*, Vol. I: *Earliest Christianity to 1453*, Maryknoll: Orbis, 2001; Vol. II: *Modern Christianity from 1453–1800*, Maryknoll: Orbis, 2012.

The Joint Declaration on the Doctrine of Justification. Grand Rapids: Eerdmans, 2000.

Jonson, Jonas. *Wounded Visions: Unity, Justice, and Peace in the World Church after 1968*. Grand Rapids: Eerdmans, 2013.

———. *Nathan Söderblom: Called to Serve*. Grand Rapids: Eerdmans, 2016.

Kasper, Walter. *The Catholic Church: Nature, Reality and Mission*. London: Bloomsbury T & T Clark, 2015.

———. *Harvesting the Fruits: Basic Aspects of Christian Faith in Ecumenical Dialogue*. London: Continuum, 2009.

———. *Luther: An Ecumenical Perspective*. New York: Paulist, 2016.

Kelly, Gerard. *Recognition: Advancing Ecumenical Thinking*. American University Studies, Series VII, 186. New York: Peter Lang, 1996.

Kinnamon, Michael. "Assessing the Ecumenical Movement." In *A History of the Ecumenical Movement: Volume 3, 1968–2000*, edited by John Briggs, Mercy Amba Oduyoye, and George Tsetsis, 51–81. Geneva: World Council of Churches, 2004.

Kinnamon, Michael, ed. *The Ecumenical Movement: An Anthology of Key Texts and Voices*. 2d ed. Geneva: World Council of Churches, 1997.

———. *Towards Visible Unity: Commission on Faith and Order*. Geneva: World Council of Churches, 1982.

Koch, Kurt. "Il Pontifico Consiglio per la Promozione dell'Unita dei Cristiani: Sviluppi et efide dell'ecumenismo." Rome: Centro Pro Unione—Semi Annual Bulletin 81 (Spring 2012) 3–12.

———. *Information Service of the Pontifical Council for Promoting Christian Unity*. 148 (2016) 36–47.

Lee, Randall, and Jeffrey Gros, FSC, eds. *The Church as Koinonia of Salvation: Its Structures and Ministries: Lutherans and Catholics X*. Washington, DC: United States Conference of Catholic Bishops, 2005.

Legrand, Hervé, OP. "Receptive Ecumenism and the Future of Ecumenical Dialogue—Privileging Differentiated Consensus and Drawing Its Institutional Consequences." In *Receptive Ecumenism and the Call to Catholic Learning*, edited by Paul Murray, 385–98. Oxford: Oxford University Press, 2008.

BIBLIOGRAPHY

Lehmann, Karl, Michael Root, and William G. Rusch, eds. *Justification by Faith: Do the Sixteenth Century Condemnations Still Apply?* New York: Continuum, 1997.

Lehmann, Karl, and Wolfhart Pannenberg, eds. *The Condemnations of the Reformation Era: Do They Still Divide?* Minneapolis: Fortress, 1999.

Leuenberg Agreement. In *An Invitation to Action: The Lutheran-Reformed Dialogue, Series III, 1981–1983,* edited by James E. Andrews and Joseph A. Burgess, 65. Philadelphia: Fortress, 1984.

Lossky, Nicholas, José Míguez Bonino, John Pobee, Thomas Stransky, Geoffrey Wainwright, and Pauline Webb, eds. *Dictionary of the Ecumenical Movement.* 2d ed. Geneva: World Council of Churches, 2002.

Maffeis, Angelo. *Ecumenical Dialogue.* Collegeville, MN: Liturgical, 2005.

McNeill, John Thomas. "The Ecumenical Idea and Efforts to Realize It, 1517–1618." In *A History of the Ecumenical Movement, 1517–1948,* 2d ed., edited by Ruth Rouse and Stephen Charles Neill, 25–69. Philadelphia: Westminster, 1967.

Meyer, Harding. "Ecumenical Consensus: Our Quest for and the Emerging Structures." *Gregorianum* 77.2 (1996) 213–25.

———. "Einheit in Versöhnter Verschiedenheit: konztiliare Gemeinschaft— 'organische Union.'" *Ökumenische Rundschau* 27 (1978) 377–400.

———. "Evangelische Teilhabe am Episkopat?" *Stimmen der Zeit* 4 (2005) 244–56; and in translation as "Differentiated Participation: The Possibility of Protestant Sharing in the Historic Office of Bishop," *Ecumenical Trends* 34.9 (2005) 9–15.

———. "'. . . 'genuinam atque integram substantiam Mysterii eucharistici non servasse . . .'? Plädoyer für eine gemeinsame Erklärung zum Verständnis des Herrenmahls." In *Kirche in ökumenischer Perspektive,* edited by Peter Walter, Klaus Klrämer, and George Augustin, 405–16. Freiburg: Herder, 2003.

———. "Konsens und Kirchengemeinschaft." *Keryma und Dogma* 31 (1985) 174–200.

———. "Die Prägung einer Formel: Ursprung und Intention." In *Einheit— über Wie? Zur Tragfähigkeit der ökumenischen Formel vom "differenzierten Konsens,"* edited by Harald Wagner, 36–58. Frieburg: Herder, 2000.

———. "Der Sich Abzeichnende Evangelische/Katholische Konsens in Theologische Verständnis des Euchariste und die Frage der Euchariste-Gemeinschaft." *Zeitschrift für Katholische Theologie* 17 (2005) 165–82.

———. *That All May be One: Perceptions and Models of Ecumenicity.* Grand Rapids: Eerdmans, 1999.

Meyer, Harding, and Lukas Vischer, eds. *Growth in Agreement: Reports and Agreed Statements of Ecumenical Conversations on the World Level.* New York: Paulist and Geneva: World Council of Churches, 1985.

Murray, Paul D., ed. *Receptive Ecumenism and the Call to Catholic Learning: Exploring a Way for Contemporary Ecumenism.* Oxford: Oxford University Press, 2008.

Nüssel, Friederike. "Ist eine 'Gemeinsame Erklärung zum Herrenmahl' möglich und sinnvoll? Überlegungen aus evangelischer Sicht." *Ökumenische Rundschau* 61 (2012) 429–39.

Pannenberg, Wolfhart. "Unity of the Church—Unity of Mankind: A Critical Appraisal of a Shift in Ecumenical Direction." *Midstream* 32.4 (October 1980) 485–90.

Quanbeck, Warren A. *Search for Understanding: Lutheran Conversations with Reformed, Anglican, and Roman Catholic Churches.* Minneapolis: Augsburg, 1972.

Rahner, Karl. "Is Church Union Dogmatically Possible?" *Theological Investigations* XVII, 197–214. New York: Crossroad, 1981.

Report of the Joint Lutheran-Roman Catholic Study Commission on "The Gospel and the Church," 1972 ("Malta Report"). In *Growth in Agreement: Reports and Agreed Statements of Ecumenical Conversations on the World Level,* edited by Harding Meyer and Lukas Vischer, 168–89. New York: Paulist and Geneva: World Council of Churches, 1985.

Report of the Section on Unity of the Third Assembly of the World Council of Churches, New Delhi, 1961. In *The Ecumenical Movement: An Anthology of Key Texts and Voices,* 2d ed., edited by Michael Kinnamon, 82–84. Geneva: World Council of Churches, 1997.

Reports of Forum on Bilateral Conversations. Geneva: World Council of Churches, 2012.

Rouse, Ruth, and Stephen Charles Neill, eds. *A History of the Ecumenical Movement, 1517–1948,* 2nd ed. Philadelphia: Westminster, 1967.

Rusch, William G. "Declaration on the Way: Church, Ministry and Eucharist: Quo Vadis?" *Ecumenical Trends* 45.5 (May 2016) 1–5, 14–15.

———. *Ecumenical Reception: Its Challenge and Opportunity.* Grand Rapids: Eerdmans, 2007.

———. *Ecumenism—A Movement toward Church Unity.* Philadelphia: Fortress, 1985.

———. "The History, Methodology, and Implications of *The Apostolicity of the Church.*" In *Towards Unity: Ecumenical Dialogue 500 Years after the Reformation,* edited by Donald Bolen, Nicholas Jesson, and Donna Geernaert, SC, 118–34. New York: Paulist, 2017.

———. "Introduction to the American Edition." In *From Conflict to Communion: Lutheran-Catholic Common Commemoration of the Reformation in 2017,* 4–7. Grand Rapids: Eerdmans, 2017.

———. *"Leuenberg Agreement."* In *The Encyclopedia of Christianity,* edited by Erwin Fahlbusch, et al., Vol. 3, 245–47. Grand Rapids: Eerdmans and Leiden: Brill, 1999–2008.

———. *Reception: An Ecumenical Opportunity.* Geneva: Lutheran World Federation, *Report* 22 and Philadelphia: Fortress Press, 1988; *Rezeption: Eine ökumenishe Chance.* Stuttgart: *Lutherische Weltbund, Report 32,* 1988.

———. "'Recognition' as an Ecumenical Concept in the Lutheran-Episcopal Dialogue." *Midstream,* 30.4 (1991) 316–22.

———. "Tradition: Lutheran." In *The Oxford Handbook of Ecumenical Studies*, edited by Geoffrey Wainwright and Paul McPartlan. Oxford: Oxford University Press, forthcoming.

———. "What is Keeping the Churches Apart?" *Ecumenical Trends* 32.1 (January 2003) 1–4.

Rusch, William G., and Daniel F. Martensen, eds. *The Leuenberg Agreement and Lutheran-Reformed Relations—Evaluations by North American and European Theologians*. Minneapolis: Augsburg, 1989.

Rush, Ormond. *The Reception of Doctrine: An Appropriation of Hans Jauss' Reception Aesthetics and Literary Hermeneutics*. Testi Gregorina, Serie Teologia 19. Rome: Editrice Pontificia Universita Gregoriana, 1997.

Ryan, Thomas, "Reception: Unpacking the New Holy Word." *Ecumenical Trends* 82 (1983) 127–34.

Saarinen, Risto. "Porvoo Common Statement." In *The Encyclopedia of Christianity*, edited by Erwin Fahlbusch, et al., Vol. 4, 290–93. Grand Rapids: Eerdmans and Leiden/Boston: Brill, 1999–2008.

Sattler, Dorothea. "Auf dem Weg zu einer 'Gemeinsamen Erklärung zum Herrenmahl?' Eine offene Frage im Für und Wider." *Ökumensiche Rundschau* 61 (2012) 411–28.

Schmidt, Martin. "Ecumenical Activity on the Continent of Europe in the Seventeenth and Eighteenth Centuries." In *A History of the Ecumenical Movement, 1517–1948*, 2d ed., edited by Ruth Rouse and Stephen Charles Neill, 71–120. Philadelphia: Westminster, 1967.

Skillrud, Harold C., Francis Stafford, and Daniel F. Martensen, eds. *Scripture and Tradition: Lutherans and Catholics in Dialogue IX*. Minneapolis: Augsburg, 1995.

Skydagaard, Kristen E., ed. *The Papal Council and the Gospel: Protestant Theologians Evaluate the Coming Vatican Council*. Minneapolis: Augsburg, 1961.

Stanley, Brian. *The World Missionary Conference, Edinburgh 1910*. Grand Rapids: Eerdmans, 2009.

Stransky, Tom. "Christian World Communinons." In *Dictionary of the Ecumenical Movement*, 2d ed., edited by Nicholas Lossky, José Míguez Bonino, John Pobee, Thomas Stransky, Geoffrey Wainwright, and Pauline Webb, 174–75. Geneva: World Council of Churches, 2002.

Sykes, Norman. "Ecumenical Movements in Great Britain in the Seventeenth and Eighteenth Centuries." In *A History of the Ecumenical Movement, 1517–1948*, 2d ed., edited by Ruth Rouse and Stephen Charles Neill, 121–67. Philadelphia: Westminster, 1967.

Tanner, Norman, SJ, ed. *Decrees of the Ecumenical Councils*. 2 vols. London and Washington, DC: Sheed & Ward and Georgetown University Press, 1990.

Tatlow, Tissington. "The World Conference on Faith and Order." In *A History of the Ecumenical Movement, 1517–1948*, 2d ed., edited by Ruth Rouse and Stephen Charles Neill, 425–41. Philadelphia: Westminster, 1967.

BIBLIOGRAPHY

The Theology of Marriage and the Problem of Mixed Marriages. In *Growth in Agreement: Reports and Agreed Statements of Ecumenical Conversations on the World Level*, edited by Harding Meyer and Lukas Vischer, 279–306. New York: Paulist and Geneva: World Council of Churches, 1985.

Thönissen, Wolfgang, ed. *"Unitatis redintegratio": 40 Jahre Ökumenismusdekret— Erbe und Auftrag*. Paderborn: Bonifatius and Frankfurt am Main: Otto Lembeck, 2005.

Tillard, Jean-Marie. "Reception: A Time to Beware of False Steps." *Ecumenical Trends* 14 (1985) 145–48.

Tjørhom, Ola. "The Demise of Visible Unity: Challenges in the Implementation of the Anglican-Lutheran Porvoo Statement." *Pro Ecclesia* XXVII (Winter 2018) 70–80.

Tjørhom, Ola, ed. *Apostolicity and Unity: Essays on the Porvoo Common Statement*. Grand Rapids: Eerdmans, 2002.

Together in Mission and Ministry: The Porvoo Statement with Essays on Church and Ministry in Northern Europe. London: Church of England, 1993.

Tomkins, Oliver Stratford. "The Roman Catholic Church and the Ecumenical Movement, 1910–1948." In *A History of the Ecumenical Movement, 1517– 1948*, 2d ed., edited by Ruth Rouse and Stephen Charles Neill, 675–93. Philadelphia: Westminster, 1967.

Unitatis Redintegratio. In *Decrees of the Ecumenical Councils*, II, edited by Norman Tanner, 908–20. London and Washington, DC: Sheed & Ward and Georgetown University Press, 1990.

Velati, Mauro. *Separati ma Fratelli: Gli Osservatori non Catholici al Vaticano II (1962–1965)*. Bologna: Il Mulino, 2014.

Vischer, Lukas. "The Ecumenical Movement and the Roman Catholic Church." In *A History the Ecumenical Movement: Vol. 2, 1948–1968*, edited by Harold E. Fey, 311–52. Philadelphia: Westminster, 1970.

Vischer 279–306. New York/Ramsey: Paulist and Geneva: World Council of Churches, 1985.

Visser 't Hooft, Willem A. *The Genesis and Formation of the World Council of Churches*. Geneva: World Council of Churches, 1982.

———. "The Genesis of the World Council of Churches." In *A History of the Ecumenical Movement, 1517–1948*, 2d ed., edited by Ruth Rouse and Stephen Charles Neill, 697–724. Philadelphia: Westminster, 1967.

———. *Has the Ecumenical Movement a Future?* Belfast: Christian Journals Limited, 1974.

Wagner, Harald, ed. *Einheit—über Wie? Zur Tragfähigkeit der ökumenischen Formel vom "differenzierten Konsens."* Freiburg: Herder, 2000.

Wainwright, Geoffrey, and Paul McPartlan, eds. *Oxford Handbook of Ecumenical Studies*. Oxford: Oxford University Press, forthcoming.

Walter, Peter, Klaus Krämer, and George Augustin, eds. *Kirche in ökumenischer Perspektive*. Freiburg: Herder:2003.

BIBLIOGRAPHY

Wenz, Gunther. "Skizze des Entwurfs einer Gemeinsamen Erklärung zur Lehre vom Herrenmahl." *Grundfragen ökumenischer Theologie, Gesammelte Aufsätze,* vol. 2, 352–63. Göttingen: Vanderhoeck & Ruprecht, 2010.

Wolfinger, Franz. "Die Rezeption theologischer Einsichten und ihre theologische und ökumenische Bedeutung: Von der Einsicht zur Verwirklung." *Catholica* 37 (1997) 202–33.

Yoder, Donald Herbert. "Christian Unity in Nineteenth Century America." In *A History of the Ecumenical Movement, 1517–1948,* 2d ed., edited by Ruth Rouse and Stephen Charles Neill, 221–59. Philadelphia: Westminster, 1967.

Index